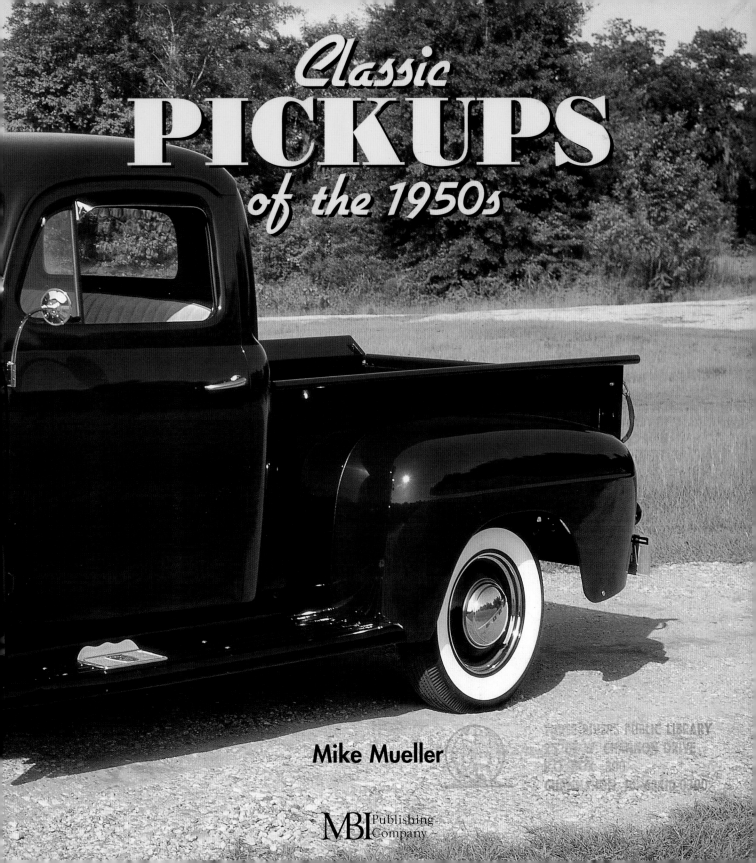

Classic PICKUPS
of the 1950s

Mike Mueller

MBI Publishing Company

First published in 1999 by MBI Publishing Company, 729 Prospect Avenue, PO Box 1, Osceola, WI 54020-0001 USA

MBI Publishing Company books are also available at discounts in bulk quantity for industrial or sales-promotional use. For details write to Special Sales Manager at Motorbooks International Wholesalers & Distributors, 729 Prospect Avenue, PO Box 1, Osceola, WI 54020-0001 USA.

Library of Congress Cataloging-in-Publication Data

Mueller, Mike
    Classic pickups of the 1950's / Mike Mueller
    p. cm. (Enthusiast color series)
    Includes index.
    ISBN 0-7603-0586-2 (pbk. : alk. paper)
    1. Pickup trucks–United States–History.
    I. Title. II. Series
TL230.5P49M4823 1999
629.223'2–dc21   99-28953

On the front cover: Bow-Tie and Blue-Oval pickups dominated the sales race during the 1950s thanks in part to these two major milestones—Chevrolet's 1955 Task Force truck (left) and Ford's 1953 F-100 (right). Owners are Kenneth Craig (Chev), of Lakeland, Florida, and Earl Lane (Ford) of Plant City, Florida.

On the frontispiece: Although quite rare, automatic transmissions began appearing on pickup option lists during the 1950s. Dearborn's truck builders first offered its Ford-O-Matic transmission for its lightest trucks in 1953. The emblem shown here graces a 1956 automatic-equipped F-100, owned by Mark Hanson of Hartseile, Alabama.

On the title page: Ford's fabled F-1, introduced in 1948, rolled on in nearly identical fashion up through 1952, then was superseded by the even more historic F-100. F-1 Fords in 1951 and 1952 can be readily identified by a new grille. But only a few minor brightwork adjustments set a 1950 F-1 apart from its forerunners. This 1950 F-1 is owned by Jim Miller of Millbrook, Alabama.

On the back cover: Dodge pickups in the early 1950s featured a black cargo box regardless of the color of the cab. A monochromatic scheme for cab and bed was optional. This 1952 B-series pickup is owned by Dwight Tew, of Franklin, Tennessee.

Edited by Paul Johnson

Designed by Dan Perry

Printed in Hong Kong

Contents

Acknowledgments

There are many people to thank for their support and involvement in this project. Various family members have always opened their doors to me during my many photo junkets. Loads of thanks go to my parents Jim and Nancy Mueller, my sister and her husband, Kathy and Frank Young, and brothers Dave and Jim Jr., all in the Champaign, Illinois, area. Also in Champaign is my good friend Ray Quinlan, who is always there whenever I come looking for help.

The list of other not-so-little people who made this mini-epic possible includes automotive historian Robert Ackerson in Schenevus, New York; literature collector/dealer Walter Miller in Syracuse, New York; and Barbara Fronczak and Lou De Simone at the Chrysler Historical Collection in Detroit. Each supplied many wonderful pieces of supportive artwork for this and other projects.

Studebaker historian Richard Quinn, in Mokena, Illinois, helped me locate various fabulous Studes to pose for my Hasselblad. Of great help, too, were all the friendly folks from two particular American Truck Historical Society membership groups—the Black Swamp Chapter, based in Fremont, Ohio, and the North Georgia Chapter. Many other nice people across the country welcomed me onto their property for various photo shoots with the various classic trucks. I can't name you all, but I do hope you like what you now see.

As for those trucks, none of this at all would have been possible without the cooperation and patience of the men and women who chose to share them with me. And you. In general order of appearance, these proud owners are:

1927 Ford Model T, Bill Broughton, Willington, Alabama; 1921 Ford Model TT one-ton, Andy and Phyllis Gray, Colfax, North Carolina; 1918 Dodge Screenside, Roy Brister, Sacramento, California; 1934 Dodge, James Ayres, Fremont, Ohio; 1918 Chevrolet Model 490, Tom Snivley, Walterville, Ohio; 1937 Studebaker

Coupe Express, Richard Stewart, Crete, Illinois; 1939 International, George Schroyer, Celina, Ohio; 1948 Diamond T Model 201, Bob and Alice Bageant, Bluefield, Virginia; 1950 Studebaker, Ken Burton, Rockford, Illinois; 1940 Studebaker Coupe-Pickup, Glen and Vera Reints, Lynwood, Illinois; 1956 Ford F-100, Mark Harrison, Hartselle, Alabama; 1966 Ford F-100, L.Q. Harrison, Hartselle, Alabama; 1957 Dodge Sweptside and 1996 Dodge Ram Indy Pace Truck, Jim Elser, Smyrna, Georgia; 1954 Chevrolet 3100, Frank Senkbeil, Cleveland, Georgia; 1970 Chevrolet, Larry Bailey, Cleveland, Georgia; 1950 Federal M-15 one-ton, Richard Walters, Fremont, Ohio; 1950 Ford F-1, Jim Miller, Millbrook, Alabama; 1951 Ford F-1, J.R. Morton, Lilburn, Georgia; 1950 GMC 3/4-ton, Roger and Eileen Bridges, Windsor, Illinois; 1952 Dodge, Dwight Tew, Franklin, Tennessee; 1954 Dodge, Dan and Beth Schaffer, St. Paul, Minnesota; 1953 Ford F-100, Mike Hauser, Metropolis, Illinois; 1955 Chevrolets (pair), 1st and 2nd series, Rich New, Adairsville, Georgia; 1957 Chevrolet 3200, Terry Adreon, Bloomington, Illinois; 1956 Chevrolet Cameo, Bob and Linda Ogle, Champaign, Illinois; 1955 Chevrolet Cameo, Olin Hoover, Lexington, South Carolina; 1957 Chevrolet Cameo, Troy Robertson, Huntersville, North Carolina; 1958 Chevrolet Cameo, Dennis and LuAnn Justi, St. Petersburg, Florida; 1953 Dodge Spring Special, Val Weakley, Greenwood, Indiana; 1957 Dodge Power Wagon, Bruce Welle, Sauk Center, Minnesota; 1957 Ford Ranchero (front view), Ron Fisher, Indianapolis, Indiana; 1957 Ford Ranchero (rear view), Dick Stern, Rancho Palos Verdes, California; and 1959 Chevrolet El Camino, Doug Stapleton, Bradenton, Florida, 1957 Dodge Sweptside (rear view), Dan Topping, Tifton, Georgia.

Thank you each and every one.

—*Mike Mueller*

Chapter 1

As American As It Gets
Introducing Our Trucking Legacy

So much history, so little time. Decades typically encompass 10 years, but it's hard to believe the 1950s only lasted that long. Nineteen-sixty still hasn't arrived for many nostalgic baby-boomers and probably won't as long as Elvis continues to haunt convenience stores across the land. That, however, is another story. The tale to be told here hinges on how one decade alone could have seen so much change, so much progression, so much expansion—not all of it positive.

Paranoia and puritanical pessimism reached all new heights during those so-called happy days. Yet sanity somehow prevailed. Riders on the 1950's roller coaster managed to survive Cold War "brinkmanship" and commie-crazed McCarthyism. Our national morality wasn't corrupted by rock 'n' roll and *Playboy* magazine as predicted. And the New York Yankees finally did surrender baseball's annual pennant race to the rest of the American League. Okay, television killed off the radio stars, but who's still around to complain?

How many Americans today still claim life here was better before suburban sprawl and upward mobility broadened our horizons? Most of us no longer know any different. Who could have imagined an America without smog, rampant road rage, and six-lane rush-hour parking lots? Certainly no one born after the 1950s.

Then again, who in 1950 could have imagined cars and trucks peacefully coexisting in the same garages, on the same boulevards, parked outside of the same restaurants and office buildings? Among the many radical changes that took root in the 1950s, one involved the way Americans looked at their four-wheeled transportation. Simply getting from point A to B evolved into arriving at point B with new found style and flair, something only the luxury car-driving elite had experienced before. In 1955, Chevrolet truly turned things upside down by introducing real prestige and performance to Average Joe and the rest of the car-buying masses in the low-priced class. That same year, Chevy also demonstrated that the good ol' American pickup truck didn't have to be a dull, plodding workhorse.

You would have to look long and hard to find something more American than the pickup truck. Baseball and apple pie don't even come close. Not

In 1925, Ford was the first to offer Americans a light-duty, steel-bodied pickup truck complete from the factory. The "Model T Runabout with Pick-Up Body" was an instant hit. This fine example is a 1927 model.

Ford's truck legacy dates back to 1917 when the Model TT one-ton chassis was introduced. Like all early trucks, Model TT tonners were sold without beds or cabs. Bodywork like that found on this 1921 Model TT was custom-built, either by an owner or one of the many pre-Depression aftermarket body-builders.

only did this country create the pickup in essence but also in being. The pickup, in turn, did more than its fair share to help create this country, or at least help make it what it is today. All along as our fast-paced, modern world was changing, progressing, and expanding, the trusty half-ton truck and its 3/4-ton big brother were there to carry the load, to haul the goods, to pull their weight. Suburbia owes its existence as much to the many pickups that were loaded down with aluminum siding for all those identical split-level homes as it does to the smog-belching Chevy Bel Airs and Ford Ranch Wagons that made commuting from the sticks to downtown possible.

No one knows exactly when the term pickup was first spoken, and an exact birthdate for this type of truck isn't simple to pin down. Pickup history is somewhat murky in that almost all early examples seen before 1930 were custom-built creations. The factory supplied a beefed-up frame, then it was left to the customer to install a cargo box or cab. Cabs and boxes were built by the customer or one of many aftermarket body-building companies that sprang up prior to World War I. Adding to the murkiness was the fact that these hybrid half-tons were also few and far between. Truly heavy haulers dominated the truck market early on. As late as the 1920s, these big, brawny brutes were still outnumbering primitive pickups by a 10-to-1 margin.

Most manufacturers called their earliest light trucks "express delivery" models, or simply "express." "Pickup" apparently evolved from street slang, with the reasoning behind its emergence being fairly obvious. When Reo label makers around 1915 were trying to promote their latest trucks, known then for their cutting-edge swiftness, they opted for the name "Hurry-Up Wagon." Once they hit the road at upwards of 30 miles per hour, these legendary haulers quickly became known by an easier off-the-tongue moniker: Speed Wagon. As fate would have it, no curbside kibitzer could ever displace the first commonly accepted generic description for any light-duty truck that could easily pick up a load and hurry it on its way.

Studebaker was among the earliest to officially use "pickup," this coming in a 1913 sales brochure. "Pick-up" was actually the common construction when printed by others at the time, and that's what International used in 1921 when describing its new S-series trucks. Popularity of the term, with hyphen, then took root in the 1930s, which was only right since that was when the American pickup truck truly began to flourish.

Ford is commonly credited with introducing the breed as we know it today because it was the first to offer a factory-built, steel-bodied, half-ton truck. Introduced in 1925, Dearborn's "Model T

The Dodge Brothers firm began building trucks in the latter half of 1917. Identified as 1918 models, these light-duty haulers were called "Screensides" for obvious reasons. Roll-up canvas curtains could protect the goods from the weather, such as the California sun shower that peppers this 1918 Screenside.

Runabout with Pick-Up Body" did away with the middlemen who had previously supplied cabs and beds. Another "factory-built" pickup, this one from Dodge Brothers, had actually appeared the year before, but it apparently failed to qualify for milestone status due to various technicalities. This 3/4-ton truck featured a wooden body supplied by the Graham Brothers firm, Dodge's Indiana-based "truck division," and was barely noticed by the truck-buying public. Only about 500 were built in 1924, compared to the 30,000 Model T pickups sold in 1925.

By 1930, Dodge, now a division of Chrysler, was offering a comparable all-steel, half-ton

Chrysler bought Dodge Brothers in 1928 and soon afterward began building complete, all-steel half-ton pickups loaded with good looks. The lines on this stylish 1934 Dodge aren't hindered in the least by a missing front bumper. The modern headlamps are also not correct.

pickup, as was Chevrolet, which just a few years before had soared out of nowhere to unseat Ford as this country's top truck manufacturer. Ford and Chevy grappled for the lead briefly in the early 1930s, then Chevy took off on a four-decade run as the number-one seller in the marketplace.

While the Big Three were staking out their territory, various independent firms also were jumping onto the pickup bandwagon in the 1930s. International's first modern half-ton appeared in 1933 by way of Willys-Overland. International simply rebadged Willys' new pickup, which had debuted in 1931. In 1937,

Studebaker rolled out its first pickup by grafting a cargo box to its Dictator automobile, copying a concept Hudson had unveiled in classy fashion three years previously.

Those car-based creations from Hudson and Studebaker represented the closest early pickups got to crossing over the fence between the work-a-day world of the truck and the fast lane of the automobile. Mixing and matching car and truck roles wasn't even considered before World War II. Trucks were trucks and cars were cars. Period. But that was then.

Once relegated primarily to the barn lot or the construction site, light-duty trucks have since left the all-work/no-play world behind and taken their place in the American automotive mainstream. Most pickups today are loaded down with as much class, comfort, and convenience as many cars—and they work as hard as ever. Snobs can chortle all they want about certain "redneck" aspects of pickup ownership. Thanks to the sky-rocketing popularity of its sport-utility brethren, the modern truck is poised to surpass its automobile counterpart in Detroit's annual sales race for the first time in history. In many homes, the traditional two-car family has been transformed into the two-truck family.

Market analysts agree Americans' need for passenger cars will never disappear. But at present, more and more buyers are relying on sport-utility vehicles and pickups as their primary mode of daily transportation. On the flipside, various once-popular automobile lines—General Motors' F-body Camaro and Firebird for instance—are teetering on the brink of extinction. Although purists may be screaming bloody murder, they had every chance to foresee this situation. Motions toward a truck-dominated market didn't just spring up overnight; they have been long in coming.

The fence between car and truck first began falling down almost a half-century ago, though it was slow going at first. The multi-role concept

Chevrolet's first trucks appeared in 1918. Both a one-ton Model T and this half-ton Model 490 were offered that first year. Typically, bodywork was added outside the factory. Complete all-steel Chevy pickups began appearing in the 1930s.

taken for granted today still remained all but undiscovered in the early 1960s. A pickup in 1960 was still a pickup: hard-working, no-nonsense, tough as nails. The wheels of progress, however, were clearly in motion.

Along the way during the 1950s, light trucks began picking up various comforts of home previously reserved for the car-buying crowd as comfort and convenience both became prominent selling points for truck dealers. A third enticement, one far easier to notice, also gained serious prominence in the 1950s. Even though

In 1937, Studebaker got into the pickup game with its Coupe Express, a stylish light truck based on the company's Dictator automobile. These beautiful haulers were built for three years only.

comfort and convenience gains were made with the first new postwar pickups, which initially emerged courtesy of Chevrolet in 1947, the primary exterior package remained one of spartan utility. Plain brown (or black, or gray, or dark green) wrapper styling continued to dominate the pickup palette. Various spruce-ups were highly touted, most laudably from Studebaker in 1949. But for the most part, the postwar pickup scheme of things still involved form taking a distant back seat to function.

Studebaker's breakthrough body wasn't one-upped until Ford introduced its new F-l00 in 1953. Chevrolet then blew everyone away with its eye-catching Task Force trucks early in 1955. But Chevrolet didn't stop there. Unveiled along with the new Task Force line was a flagship that alone

Veteran truck maker International Harvester began offering pickups in 1933, with these first models being rebadged Willys-Overland models. International phased in its own light truck within a few years. This is a 1939 D-2 half-ton.

did more than any other truck to help change the way Americans looked at their pickups.

If any one pickup can be called the forerunner of today's multi-talented, "truck-about-town" utility vehicles, it is Chevy's Cameo Carrier. The Cameo definitely changed all the rules, at least from a truck-builder's perspective. Giving greater attention to styling was one thing; creating a truly classy image for a pickup certainly never had been done before—and

probably hasn't been matched in relative degree since. Still very much a typical half-ton truck beneath that beautiful skin, the Cameo nonetheless impressed its audiences with a polite persona that, for the first time ever, paired the terms prestige and pickup.

Chevrolet offered the Cameo Carrier in decreasing numbers only up into 1958. Success in this case, however, should not be measured by sales figures or longevity, it is best judged by

Renowned for its big trucks, Diamond T began offering pickups in the 1930s. The one-ton Model 201, introduced in 1938, carried on almost unchanged until 1949, when it was replaced by the less-popular Model 222. Nearly all Diamond T pickups were painted red, like this 1948 Model 201.

Studebaker went from quick-fix to cutting edge in less than 10 years. In 1940 (right), it was marketing cars equipped with optional trunk-mounted cargo boxes. In 1949, the stylish 2R Studebaker pickup established new standards for light-truck design. The 2R at left is a 1950 model.

impact. The pickup market was never the same again after the Cameo's debut. Chevy had demonstrated what a little class could do for pickup popularity, and the lesson learned was not lost on the competition.

Ford responded to the Cameo's challenge with two new models in 1957. The first was the Styleside pickup, which borrowed the Cameo's smooth bedsides theme and reformed it in steel. Chevy then responded in turn in 1958 with its

Fleetside, a stylish, steel-boxed truck that picked up where the Cameo left off. Dodge too joined the trendy cab-wide bed club in 1959 with its attractive Sweptline rendition.

Dearborn's other new-for-1957 product was the Ranchero, a unique variation on the classy utility vehicle theme. Instead of adding car-line touches to a truck, Ford designers simply transformed a car into a pickup. Chevy then tried the same trick in 1959.

THEN

Studebaker rounds out its first century
on the roadways of the world

Even the Pony Express was a long way off—eight years in the future, in fact—when America's first Studebaker swung upon the scene.

Gold had just been discovered in California—and two young Indiana blacksmiths named Henry and Clem Studebaker saw opportunity in it.

They felt that people heading West would need a lot of wagons. They decided to build some. How right their judgment was is borne out by history. America's most dynamic period of expansion and development was about to get going.

The little $68 wagon shop the Studebaker brothers opened up in 1852 is now the world's fourth largest automotive vehicle manufacturing enterprise. It does a business of more than half a billion dollars a year.

The pages of this folder illustrate and describe some of the notable high spots in Studebaker's first 100 years on the roadways of the world. But like a vigorous young redwood a century of age, Studebaker has only started growing.

STUDEBAKER TRUCKS

Noted for low-cost operation

NOW

"But like a vigorous young redwood a century of age, Studebaker has only started growing." Who was kidding whom? Studebaker celebrated its 100th birthday in 1952 just in time to kick off its downward skid into oblivion.

So which came first, the chicken or the egg? Did truck buyers in the 1950s suddenly discover that they wanted comfortable, convenient, classy pickups? Or did Detroit convince them of such? Did supply meet demand? Or was it the magic of modern marketing? The latter is probably the best answer even though the product promotion tactics we know and love (or is that loathe?) today were then just as new as the products themselves. Progress in advertising was only natural in the 1950s given the proliferation of products to be advertised, all a result of the sellers' market that instantly developed in 1946 when a goods-hungry population was reunited with a mass-production-crazed private sector made private again once World War II was won.

Better living then became the big goal of the 1950s; better living through chemicals, better living through affordable prefabricated homes, better living through automation. According to

Okay, Chevy's Task Force trucks were tough, but would you torture your Cameo Carrier like this? Introduced in 1955, the Cameo helped set the stage for the appearance of today's high-class haulers.

automakers, bigger was better and biggest was best. New was naturally better, so new alone soon wasn't good enough—it had to be new and improved. At the same time, need was quickly superseded by want. The better the living got, the more living we wanted. The more we wanted, the more the market was willing to give us. We may never have needed more comfortable, more convenient, more classy pickup trucks. But by the time the 1950s came to an end, we wanted them like never before.

The total truck market itself did not experience any major transformation as a result of these changing attitudes. Americans may have begun preferring nicer pickups 40-something years ago, but any real thoughts of trading the daily-driver automobile for a light truck at the time remained to be thunk. No major upward spikes in the utility vehicle sales graph appeared after 1950, and in fact annual registration records, encompassing everything from pickups to big rigs, showed a downturn—1.14 million new trucks were registered in 1950; 942,000 showed up in official paperwork in 1959. Although a national recession in 1958 did have something to do with these results, it didn't change the fact that truck sales, averaging about 900,000 a year during the decade, were never a threat to the automobile's share of the total vehicle market at that time.

What the 1950s contributed most to today's trend toward a truck-dominated market was that new attitude. It was then left to pickup buyers of the 1960s to get the ball rolling faster. Trucks in 1960 made up a tidy 12.5 percent of the total market, which consisted of 7.6 million vehicles. Ten years later, that figure hit 18.9 percent, then jumped to 27.9 in 1978. The 40 percent barrier was breached in 1993, fed of course by the meteoric rise of the SUV. And, as mentioned, the 50 percent mark is being approached even as we speak. Truck sales in 1997 surpassed 7 million, an all-time high.

While no sales shifts from truck to car occurred in the 1950s, numbers did reflect

In 1953, Ford picked up the pace by introducing its milestone F-100, which continued on almost unchanged save for a wraparound windshield added in 1956 (right). F-series pickups were still turning heads 10 years later, as demonstrated by the 1966 F-100 short-bed in the background.

another historic trend. As was the case on the car side of the fence, the truck market by 1960 had experienced its fair share of homogenization. Though the pickup pie served each year since 1950 remained about the same size, the individual slices cut out of it had become noticeably larger than in previous decades as Big Three domination reached full flower. Chevrolet

(along with corporate cousin GMC), Ford and Dodge solidified their roles as the market's major players.

Actually, a better description of the situation would've been the "Big Two and Dodge." Always miles ahead of all competitors, Chevrolet and Ford teamed up to score between 53 and 68 percent of annual truck sales during the 1950s.

Dodge trucks have always played third fiddle, but at least they've always played it loud. Just as there was no missing the Indy Pace Truck in 1996, the same could have been said about the Sweptside in 1957. Passenger-car tail fins brought up the Sweptside's rear.

Chrysler's truck division dating back to the 1920s perennially ranked a far distant third, and sometimes not even that as International often pushed Dodge back to fourth. Beginning in 1954, GMC gains, combined with sagging Dodge popularity, dropped Chrysler down yet another notch for the remainder of the decade.

From a pickup perspective, however, Dodge can still be considered the long-running third-place player since light trucks have always been its meat and potatoes. International Harvester, and to a lesser extent GMC, relied much more heavily on bigger commercial vehicles.

Studebaker experienced a rapid decline during the 1950s and was all but dead by

Chevrolet was the leader of the American truck market for almost four decades and for good reason. The Advance Design models, built from 1947 to early 1955, helped get the postwar pickup jump started. The 1954 3100-series pickup shown here remained as popular as its forerunners. Chevrolet pickups in 1970 (left) were still at the leading edge as far as both form and function were concerned.

1960. Tiny Crosley, which had begun offering its truly compact pickups in 1940, was barely alive when the decade began, then finally closed the doors in 1952. Lightly regarded Willys remained relatively healthy, this thanks to its entrenchment in the then-unexplored off-road field. But that was just about that. Save for an occasional, rarely-seen rival from the likes of Diamond T or Powell, there were

no other distractions for Big Three pickup buyers in the 1950s. Plymouth, Durant, American Bantam, Reo, Mack, Federal, Stewart—of the various off-the-beaten-path pickup nameplates present and accounted for in the 1930s only Hudson survived the second World War. It too was gone after 1947.

Three years later a new decade dawned. Make that a new and improved decade.

Chapter 2

Enter the Fabulous Fifties
New Pickups for a New Decade

The American truck industry celebrated the arrival of the 1950s by establishing a new all-time high for production. As anyone could've guessed, sales of all types of vehicles quickly soared after peacetime operations resumed in 1946. New truck registrations that year, as reported by R.L. Polk & Company, reached 625,249 in 1946, compared to the 640,697 registered in the prewar record year of 1941. That standard was shattered when the R.L. Polk roll call hit 879,132 in 1947. Yet another record followed when the 1 million barrier was breached in 1948. After a slight dip in 1949, truck sales surged again to new heights, this time to 1,142,307 in 1950. Various stumbling blocks intervened to limit further sales growth in the 1950s. The police action in Korea during the decade's early years and an economic downturn in 1958 helped quiet any further booms. The million-truck plateau wasn't reached

again until 1962, and the 1950 record was finally topped in 1963.

The economic boom following World War II deserves the lion's share of the credit for all the record-breaking sales in the car and truck industry during the late 1940s. This was especially so in the automobile market considering most of the so-called new models were thinly veiled rehashes of the same old cars sold in 1941 and briefly in 1942. Market leaders Chevrolet and Ford didn't introduce new cars on the market until 1949. It was left to the independents, perhaps because they had to try harder, to initially introduce war-weary Americans to modern automobiles. In 1947, Studebaker shocked Detroit (and offered no apologies to 1946's new kid on the block, Kaiser-Frazer) by becoming "the first by far with a postwar car." Hudson and Packard followed suit in 1948, and the next year a major

Only Chevrolet could build basically the same truck for eight years and still stay in the sales lead. In 1947, the Advance Design models emerged as this country's first new postwar pickup. This 1954 Chevy half-ton shows off the only major exterior upgrade made during the Advance Design run: a new grille. Chrome plating that grille was optional.

Pickup buyers in the postwar years had grown more interested in comfort and ease of use. Increased cab width, to better seat three adults, and an enlarged one-piece windshield, the better to see where all three were going, were main selling points of Chevrolet's Advance Design trucks.

player finally joined in as General Motors introduced its modernized Cadillac. A completely updated postwar automobile market wasn't fully in place until 1950.

Things were slightly different for the light-truck market. Outsiders may have beaten the Big Three to the punch with new postwar cars, but the opposite was true for new postwar trucks. On top of that, many of the pickups Americans were buying up like hotcakes in 1950 were already old news. Detroit not only introduced modern postwar pickups first, it did so even before most modern postwar cars were on the market. Chevrolet's Advance Design trucks wowed the working man's crowd in the summer of 1947, followed closely by similar counterparts

from GMC. Ford's F-series and Dodge's "Pilot House" pickups both made their debuts in 1948. New trucks before new automobiles? What was the story?

The simplest answer involves the obvious fact that it took more time to kick start automobile manufacturing after its wartime shutdown. Truck assembly lines, however, remained rolling during the war to supply the military with the means to carry the fight to the Germans and Japanese. Once they were defeated, gearing back up for the peacetime production of civilian-issue pickups required far less sweat. Chevy chief engineer John Woods described the situation in 1947. "Long before the war ended, the government permitted Chevrolet to begin production of trucks

Chevrolet got a leg up on Ford in 1929 by introducing a six-cylinder engine for its car and truck lines. That good old "Stovebolt" was still purring along in 1954. This 235-cid six was joined in 1955 by Chevy's first modern overhead-valve V-8.

The 4-Wheel-Drive Truck *that's different!*

Study—
these many features and advantages

1 *Four-Wheel drive:* Great tractive ability for off-the-road operation . . . impossible with a conventional 2-wheel drive truck. For highway operation, front-wheel drive can be easily disengaged from within the cab.

2 *Eight forward speeds:* From regular 4-speed transmission and a 2-speed transfer case. They offer time-saving, flexible performance, and maximum engine efficiency.

3 *Power Winch:* Available for front mounting, provides 7,500 lbs. pulling or hoisting capacity. Complete with 250 ft. of ⅜ inch steel cable, automatic safety brake, and throw-out clutch.

4 *Dual power take-off:* For front or rear operation. Provides power for a variety of on-truck and off-truck equipment. Functions at 61½% or 47½% of engine speed, depending on direction of rotation.

5 *Tail shaft drive:* Available for operation of a variety of auxiliary equipment. Can be governed at 536 r.p.m. or

other speeds if desired. Nine-inch pulley drive available for operating circular saws, silo fillers, pumps, and other belt-driven machinery.

6 *Mechanical governor:* Provides constant engine speed for power operations when needed. Conveniently controlled over a wide range of settings from inside the cab.

7 *Tow hook:* May be mounted on front of frame. Convenient for a variety of dragging or pulling operations.

8 *Pintle hook:* Available for mounting on the rear frame cross member. Adaptable for towing equipment with towing eyes, chains, or cables.

9 *Full-size enclosed cab:* Wherever you drive a POWER-WAGON, you drive in comfort. Safety-steel cab comfortably accommodates three adults . . . offers safe vision and driving convenience.

10 *Large express body:* 58 cu. ft. load capacity. Durable hardwood floor, protected by steel skid strips. Hinged tail gate has chain and hook and eye fasteners.

Here's the truck that *needs no roads* . . . the truck of *1,001 uses* . . . the truck that's *different* . . . the Dodge POWER-WAGON.

It gives you TRACTION *when* you need it . . . PULL *as* you need it . . . and POWER *where* you need it.

It's really a *power plant* on wheels! By choice of the proper auxiliary equipment you can use it for many specialized tasks to do each of those tasks better. And you'll find that it's *"Job-Rated"* for operation under widely varying and extreme conditions.

Investigate the great versatility of the Power-Wagon . . . its adaptability to so many new uses. We're sure you'll agree with thousands of users "there's no truck anywhere like the Dodge POWER-WAGON!"

While Chevrolet was the first to offer a new postwar half-ton, Dodge's one-ton 4x4 Power Wagon was actually the first new "pickup" to appear on the peacetime market. Introduced in 1946, the Power Wagon wore the same basic "army truck" uniform until 1968.

for civilians on the same lines on which military vehicles were being built," he wrote. "Hence, when the war was won, it was not necessary to reconvert lines, and continued production averted an acute truck shortage."

Ford began building a small number of utility vehicles for high-priority civilian uses in May 1944. Ford customers began taking home this country's first new trucks sold to the public since February 1942 on May 3, 1945. Dodge's civilian truck production line was also under way by then, and Chevrolet's came to life later in August. The vehicles that rolled off these lines, of course, were simply copies of the last peacetime trucks built in 1942.

Chevrolet's Advance Design model appeared in May 1947. While this was indeed America's first all-new, half-ton postwar pickup, it didn't actually qualify for the honor of first truck. That kudo was copped by Dodge more than one year before. During the war, Dodge had made a big name for itself building super-heavy-duty, all-wheel-drive (both 4x4 and 6x6) machines for the military. The company then opted to continue production of its one-ton 4x4 truck for civilian use. As legend has it, the Dodge plant began preparing to build its new Power Wagon only hours after the last military 4x4 rolled off the line. Announced in March 1946, this big, burly peacetime pickup was, according to official brochures, "the truck the boys wrote home about... now in civvies." Dodge marketed its "army truck" Power Wagon in essentially identical no-nonsense form up through 1968. The company in 1957 introduced a more civilized version wearing standard Dodge pickup sheet metal in place of that somewhat crude-looking military body with its prewar-style cab. These fashion-conscious 4x4 Power Wagons soldiered on until 1980.

That it took 10 years before Dodge offered a 4x4 pickup better suited for the mainstream market was understandable considering how lightly regarded the four-wheel-drive niche was

DESIGNED FOR TOUGH GOING
BUILT FOR LASTING STRENGTH
THE 1951 4 WHEEL DRIVE WILLYS TRUCK

Far less burly than Dodge's Power Wagon—yet no wimp—was the one-ton Jeep pickup from Willys, introduced in 1947. These 4x4s were marketed with few changes through the 1950s into the 1960s.

in the 1950s. In the early part of that decade, Ford and Chevrolet officials couldn't have cared less about off-road capability. It was possible, however, to equip their lighter trucks with four-wheel drive hardware by way of aftermarket sources. Most notable were the Napco-converted "Mountain Goat" Chevys and the Marmon–Herrington Fords, which dated back to 1936. Chevrolet finally began building its own 4x4 pickups in 1957, followed by Ford two years later.

In the meantime, it was left to another outsider to do the bulk of the off-road market's trailblazing during the 1950s. The self-proclaimed world leader in four-wheel-drive vehicle production at that time was Willys, which like Dodge had simply continued doing in peacetime what it had done so well during World War II. Before the war, Willys-Overland had built cars and stylish half-ton pickups, but these vehicles didn't return

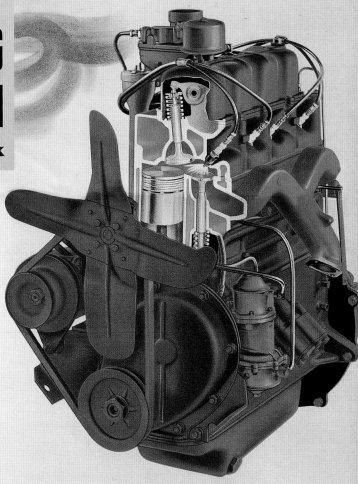

Willys-Overland's new truck engine for the 1950s was the F-head Hurricane four-cylinder. The F-head name referred to valve layout: this engine was partially a "side-valver" like an L-head (notice exhaust valve below firing spark plug), but its intake valve was mounted in modern overhead fashion.

Like Diamond T, big-truck builder Federal also dabbled in the pickup field, although its efforts at the market's lighter end came and went before World War II, with the exception of this one-of-a-kind M-15 one-ton. Undoubtedly the largest, longest pickup you'll ever see, this Federal was custom-built in 1950 by the Perfection Steel Body in Galion, Ohio, to haul tarp rolls and extension ladders for the Pfefferkorn Awning Company in Sandusky, Ohio. That big, orange bed is 14 feet long.

to production in 1946. Willys officials instead chose to load all their marbles into the back of their fabled four-wheel-drive Jeep. Production of the first civilian-issue Jeeps, the appropriately labeled "CJ" models, began in July 1945.

Willys' 1/4-ton CJ was joined by a similarly styled one-ton Jeep pickup in the summer of 1947. Some 50,000 Jeep pickups, in both 4x2 and 4x4 forms, were on the road (or off it) by 1949. Like Dodge's original Power Wagon, Jeep trucks rolled on in identical fashion through the 1950s. That familiar facade with its squared-off fenders stayed on the scene until 1963.

Another all-new, off-road vehicle, this one of the rear-wheel drive variety, appeared in 1950, just in time to help mark its parent company's final farewell. Cincinnati mogul Powel Crosley, Jr. had first offered his little "car for the forgotten man" in 1939. He then built a pickup version of the truly compact Crosley automobile in 1940. These diminutive 1/4-ton trucks carried over into the postwar market, and in 1947 became the first pickups to feature fully flush body sides in place of traditionally bulging fenders, a style that helped make Chevrolet's Cameo famous eight years later. Additional Crosley innovations

In 1948, Ford introduced its first new postwar pickup, the F-1, which was built through 1952. This 1950 F-1 shows very few updates compared to its forerunners.

included the new-for-1947 "Cobra" (for its lightweight COpper-BRAzed sheet-steel engine block) four-cylinder power plant and the industry's first disc brakes in 1949.

A third ground-breaking offering came in the form of the aforementioned new model introduced for 1950. Production of Crosley pickups had fallen to only 287 in 1949—this after sales for all models had surpassed 22,000 two years before. But that didn't stop Powel Jr. from taking one last shot at convincing Americans that they needed small, affordable, fuel-efficient cars and trucks. Maybe the forgotten man wasn't interested in his vehicles, but what about the forgotten farmer? In August 1950, Crosley introduced its Farm-O-Road truck for rural

Ford managed to beat Chevrolet to the punch in the 1950s when it came time to update its postwar pickup line. The F-1 was fitted with a restyled grille in 1951.

Ford's F-series cabs offered much the same newfound room and comfort as Chevrolet's Advance Design interiors, although its enlarged one-piece windshield wasn't quite as big as Chevy's. Also notice the typically Spartan accouterments. Specifically observe the single sun visor, for the driver only. Standard Advance Design cabs were no different.

Chevrolet introduced pickup buyers to a powerful six-cylinder engine in 1929. Ford then upped the ante to a V-8 in 1932. A revised version of that valve-in-block "flathead" V-8 was still being offered as a truck option in 1951. Displacement was 239 cubic inches.

customers looking for a cheap way to both do the chores and travel to town.

The $795 Farm-O-Road got nearly 40 miles per gallon, it reportedly hit 60 miles per hour on the highway, and it worked like no other pint-sized Crosley. It had an auxiliary gearbox with a 4.1 torque multiplication and dual rear wheels, which could be individually locked to aid turning. Options included a pickup bed with or without a hydraulic dump mechanism, front and rear power take-offs, and a hydraulic drawbar in back that could mount a wide array of mowers and farm implements. A top, side curtains and a back seat were also available.

As much as the Farm-O-Road had to offer, it never had a chance to find a niche. Crosley's fate already had been sealed. Public confidence suffered mightily due to engineering gremlins. The rust-magnet Cobra engine was unable to hold its coolant, and the company's disc brakes proved useless in the real world when dirt infiltrated them. Even after correcting these maladies, Crosley still couldn't get past a plain reality—the time for compact cars and trucks had not come to America. Meager production continued before the little firm finally closed down in July 1952. The Farm-O-Road was later revived by San Diego's Crofton Marine Engine

GMC rode the coattails of Chevrolet's success in the pickup market and commonly ranked as high as fourth in truck industry rankings during the 1950s. This 1950 GMC 3/4-ton wears a 1948 GMC grille and an owner-applied custom paint accent.

Company as the Crofton Bug. About 250 Crofton Bugs were sold between 1959 and 1962.

While dying, defiant Crosley was futilely trying to prove that less could indeed be more, the Big Three were busy demonstrating that more undoubtedly was better—more features, more advancements, more of everything that made a pickup a pickup. Reviewing Chevrolet's big, boastful Advance Design brochure in 1947 was almost akin to reading *War and Peace*. By the time the last all-new postwar pickup, International's L-series, introduced very late in 1949, was on the market, industry bragging rights had

expanded to encompass a dizzying array of supposedly dazzling details.

The more things change, the more they stay the same. Ford, Chevy, and Dodge—especially Dodge—for a number of years now haven't been able to make commercials fast enough to brag about having the latest first truck to do this or that. The first with three doors, the first with four doors, the first with ABS brakes, the first with 10 cylinders.

Fresh, trend-setting features truckmakers had been bragging about a half-century ago included larger windshields that no longer left a pickup driver feeling like a submarine captain peering through a periscope. Dodge's new postwar pickups weren't called Pilot House for nothing. Chevrolet label makers claimed the Advance Design truck's enlarged glass area afforded drivers "Observation Car Vision." Ford's F-series was fitted with a "Safety Vision Windshield" that, although smaller than rivals' front glass, was of groundbreaking one-piece construction. International one-upped Ford with its new one-piece L-series windshield by curving it ever so slightly, a truck-industry first that was then as notable as the introduction of airbags was 45 years later.

Another selling point popularized in the 1950s was the one-piece "alligator" hood, a design that actually debuted just before the war. It helped make engine access easier by hinging at the rear. While Chevrolet and GMC were especially proud of their postwar gators, International's one-piece L-series hood still opened wide to either side (your choice) in old-fashioned fashion. But its unique latching system also allowed it to disconnect completely and lift off clean out of the way.

By 1950, all pickup dealers were bragging of newfound levels of convenience. Such talk was easily drowned out, though, by the din created by advancements in an area rarely considered before—comfort. Cab designs were by the far the main topics of postwar pickup hype. Along with reportedly being safer, these reinforced, more durable cabs were clearly roomier as suddenly the need to seat three across became a priority to pickup owners. Or so they were told.

Based on "Unisteel Battleship" construction, Chevy's widened Advance Design cab offered eight more inches for hips, 3.5 inches for shoulders, and an additional foot for feet compared to its 1946 forerunner. The Pilot House Safety Cab that Dodge introduced for its new B-series pickup in 1948 was also taller, longer, and wider. Ford designers reportedly spent $1 million on ergonomic developments even before they knew what ergonomics was. Dearborn's

International was the last to introduce a new postwar pickup. The company's modernized L-series light truck line came out late in 1949. The exposed door hinges (where the mirror is mounted) helps identify this as a 1951 model; 1950 L-series pickups had hidden hinges.

"Bonus Built" (more truck for your money) F-series pickup featured the aptly named "Million Dollar Cab," with its "Living-Room" accouterments. As the last of the postwar pickup-makers to unveil a modern model, International admen feared not about touting their L-series cab as "the roomiest on the road."

Additional comfort was guaranteed by still more enhancements. Along with being expanded in all directions, Ford's F-1 cab allowed three adults to enter and exit with little fear of bruising knees, as the door hinges were moved three inches forward. Chevy's doors had been previously enlarged with passengers' knees in mind, and the Advance Design pickup also featured an easier-on-the-seat seat fitted with extra springs. Better seat springing, combined with a wider adjustment range, contributed to the F-1 interior's "Easy Chair Comfort." Ford also added its "Level Action Cab" suspension system, which relied on rubber mounts to insulate cab from frame. Dodge's B-series cab rode on rubber mounts as well, and B-series drivers themselves rode on a new "Air-O-Ride" seat that pampered bottoms with both a cushion of air and coil springs.

Major mechanical advancements for the first wave of modernized postwar pickups made nowhere near as many headlines. During the early 1950s, Chevrolet still relied on basically the same "Stovebolt" six-cylinder engine that had been introduced in 1929. A similar situation existed at Ford, where the venerable "flathead" V-8 was in its third decade of service. An antiquated L-head six continued powering Studebaker pickups throughout the 1950s but was finally joined by an optional overhead-valve

Dodge's B-series "Pilot House" pickups hit the market in 1948. They were superseded by the C-series models in 1954. This 1952 B-3-B shows off the trusty, 10-year-old "Job-Rated" motto, added to Dodge truck grilles in 1951. The black cargo box was standard. Solid-color finishes were optional.

NOW... available for the first time on conventional trucks...

NEW
Truck-o-matic Transmission

WITH gyrol FLUID DRIVE
Available on all ½- and ¾-ton models

Now...at last...truck operators can enjoy the effortless driving ease of *shift-free hauling* thanks to the new Dodge Truck-o-matic transmission!

Think of the benefits that only Dodge Truck-o-matic can give you! Benefits like hauling your loads over your roads without shifting at every intersection or grade... and full driver control that lets *you* select the right gear for conditions of the moment.

Furthermore, Dodge retains the clutch pedal for use when needed. It lets you rock your truck back and forth if stuck in deep mud or snow. And you can inch more slowly with precision into tight loading areas.

Yes... there's an entirely new driving experience waiting for you in a Dodge "*Job-Rated*" truck with Truck-o-matic transmission. Just drive one and see for yourself!

REVERSE

POWER RANGE

NEUTRAL

DRIVING RANGE

TRUCK-O-MATIC TRANSMISSION with gyrol Fluid Drive is a constant-mesh unit with four speeds forward and one reverse. Shifting up or down between the two speeds in the power range and the two speeds in normal driving range is done hydraulically, and is controlled by the accelerator pedal. Shifting between power and driving range is manually controlled.

Ask for a Demonstration Soon!

Chrysler's semi-automatic Fluid Drive equipment appeared as a Dodge truck option in 1950 and represented the truck industry's first attempt at shift-free driving. In 1953, Dodge went one step further with its Truck-O-Matic option, equipment which made the clutch even less of a pesky proposition.

V-8 in 1955. International's L-series was the only all-new postwar pickup to also come right out of the box with an all-new engine, the overhead-valve Silver Diamond six-cylinder. This powerplant superseded the Green Diamond L-head six used in 1949. International didn't begin putting V-8s in its half-ton pickups until 1959.

Ever-off-the-wall Willys introduced its new F-head Hurricane four-cylinder in 1950 for its wagon line. The 72-horse Hurricane four then found its way into Willys pickups in 1951. F-head construction featured the exhaust valve in the block while the intake valve operated overhead. With standard compression of 6.9:1 (an optional "high-altitude" head boosted that ratio to 7.4:1) the F-head Hurricane powerplant was, according to Willys' ads, the "highest compression engine in any farm truck."

Dodge roared out of the pack in 1954 with the "world's most powerful pickup," a claim supported wholeheartedly by the Chrysler light truck line's first V-8. Made available in June that year, the 24l-ci overhead-valve Power-Dome V-8 was rated at 145 horsepower. It was not a Hemi, as its name might have implied; it did not have hemispherical combustion chambers like Dodge's top car-line powerplants. Dodge truck's Power-Dome V-8 instead relied on Plymouth's "polyspherical" head design.

Along with being the first to offer real horsepower to light-truck buyers, Dodge pickups also paved the way for shiftless driving into the cargo-carrying ranks. Chrysler's Fluid Drive, a prewar development, was introduced as a pickup option in April 1950. This wasn't a true automatic transmission—a fluid coupling system simply allowed drivers to get away with foregoing clutch usage in some situations—but it was a start.

Three years later Dodge upped the ante again, this time with its Truck-O-Matic option. Truck-O-Matic combined that fluid coupling with Chrysler's M6 semi-automatic transmission. Although a clutch was still included in the deal, it was needed even less–basically only for initial launches. The two-speed M6 transmission automatically shifted up at certain speeds. Although the equipment worked nicely, its $110 asking price limited demand for its installation. Truck-O-Matic Dodge pickups were quite rare, and the option was superseded by Dodge's first true automatic transmission in 1955.

Dodge was also among the first to improve ease of use by addressing steering effort. The new B-series truck's shortened wheelbase, reduced from the previous 116-inch stretch to 108 inches, helped balance the load, both engine and cargo, better than before. Working along with a widened front track and a new cross-steering design, this shortened wheelbase markedly improved ride and handling and also made the Pilot House pickup's turning radius probably the tightest in its field. Ford relocated the first F-100's front axle in 1953 with similar results. Chevrolet in 1955 and International in 1957 altered wheelbase and front suspension location to help make steering its pickups less of a real man's job.

Fashion statements made by the first new postwar pickups still left much to be desired,

This is about as upscale as it got for pickup drivers in the early 1950s. Options present in this 1953 Dodge Spring Special cab include a deluxe heater, twin sun visors and accessory turn signals. The color is a non-stock, owner-preferred touch.

For 1954, Dodge's mildly restyled C-series pickup still shared much of the B-series basic image. The most notable addition was a one-piece curved windshield. This 1954 Dodge is fitted with the rare Truck-O-Matic option.

that is they did when judged from a modern-day perspective. As dated as it looks now, Chevrolet's Advance Design form was warmly welcomed in 1947 as a certified step forward into the thoroughly modern postwar world. Of course, truck buyers then didn't expect much since the vehicles they were buying remained fully entrenched in the all-work, no-play class. Any extra attention paid to freshening exterior impressions, however lightly, would've been appreciated 50 years ago.

Chevy's humble offerings in 1947 included headlights incorporated within the fenders instead of in pods on top, an antiquated practice

Ford had given up by 1940 and International by 1941. Dodge eliminated its pods in 1948. Chevrolet and Dodge's new postwar pickups also featured hidden door hinges, which helped make exterior lines cleaner and less cluttered. International at first hid its hinges in 1950, then revealed them again in 1951.

All the pickups introduced from 1947 to 1950 featured their share of modernized impressions. Yet beneath those updates remained the same basic pickup shell. Chevrolet, Ford, and International stuck to the existing construction formula: cabs with exposed running boards were

Power plus economy!

Power Dome V-8

powerful...
economical...dependable

This great new 169-hp. Power-Dome V-8 engine makes your Dodge *"Job-Rated"* pick-up the most powerful in the popular ½-ton field! This engine is a great successor to the Power-Dome V-8 that averaged 22 miles per gallon in AAA-supervised Economy Run. That's because unique Power-Dome combustion chambers squeeze more mileage from regular grade gas!

More power output—Power-Dome combustion chambers reduce heat loss, permit greater, more efficient expansion of gases to drive pistons.

Longer engine life—Rounded combustion chamber has no pockets for carbon build-up. Maintenance is reduced, valve life lengthened.

Type	Overhead Valve, V-8
Bore and Stroke	3.563″ x 3.25″
Displacement	259.2 cu. in.
Max. Gross Horsepower	169 @ 4400 r.p.m.
Max. Gross Torque, lbs.-ft.	243 @ 2400 r.p.m.
Compression Ratio	7.6 to 1

Thrifty Six

money maker...
money saver—on any job

For real dependability, there's the tried-and-true L-head Dodge six–a 110-hp. glutton for punishment that *saves* you money in cost of operation and maintenance. Balanced high compression ratio (7.25 to 1) assures efficient operation on regular fuel. Heavy-duty cooling system contributes to peak performance with full protection for the engine under all conditions.

Simple L-head design—Use of a minimum number of parts in this rugged, dependable engine means trouble-free performance, low maintenance.

Exhaust valve seat inserts—Extra-hard inserts protect valve seats against wear, give better valve seating and help assure longer valve life.

Type	L-head, 6-cylinder
Bore and Stroke	3.25″ x 4.625″
Displacement	230.2 cu. in.
Max. Gross Horsepower	110 @ 3600 r.p.m.
Max. Gross Torque, lbs.-ft.	194 @ 1600 r.p.m.
Compression Ratio	7.25 to 1

Dodge was the first to make a major play in the pickup power field, introducing its first V-8 in 1954. Not just any V-8, the 145-horse Power Dome engine instantly transformed Dodge's light trucks into the industry's strongest. In 1955, output grew to 169 horses.

MEMO from the desk of POWEL CROSLEY, JR.

② cuts service costs

CROSLEY

JONES APPLIANCE SERVICE

Crosley's mini-pickup barely survived into the 1950s, but it did make its mark. Unveiled in 1949, this design carried on, however feebly, until early 1952. It featured the truck industry's first "slab-side" cargo box, a style later popularized by Chevrolet's classy Cameo Carrier.

joined to crude cargo boxes, and bulbous pontoon fenders were bolted on at all four corners to keep the mud down.

Dodge may well deserve credit for being first to crack if not break that mold. The Pilot House front end in 1948 took on more of an integrated, fully styled appearance thanks to front fender tops that ventured up closer to the hoodline then flowed back into the doors of the widened cab. These fenders were not bulbous in the least and looked more like they were sculpted into the body, not merely bolted on. Running board presence, too, was minimized. A restyle for the new

C-series Dodge in 1954 enhanced these impressions even further to a point where the body almost qualified as "slabsided," a fenderless styling trend car watchers had been going ga-ga over since Hudson (again without apologies to Kaiser-Frazer) first popularized the look in 1948. Few critics made note of Dodge's new look, however, undoubtedly because fewer and fewer buyers in the 1950s were embracing Dodge's new trucks.

The same went for poor Studebaker. South Bend's once-great wagon maker was already rolling steadily into the sunset even as officials in Indiana were celebrating a century in business in

Crosley introduced its intriguing Farm-O-Road in 1950. This 1951 model shows off the towbar, power takeoff and dual rear wheels, which could be locked individually to quicken turns.

1952. In 1950, Studebaker held a decent 4 percent of the truck market. Four years later, the percentage fell to 1.2, and it was a dismal 0.57 percent by 1958. And to think this was the company that first demonstrated in a big way that pickups could have real style.

Dodge's polite progress aside, Studebaker emerged as the postwar pickup market's main mover and shaker in the styling department. The veteran independent's allegiance with Raymond Loewy's cutting-edge design studio essentially guaranteed such a result. As they had done for the car market in 1947, Studebaker planners in 1949 were hoping to wake up the utility field to an all-new era, a time when light trucks would be welcomed into the automobile's world. These trucks would work as hard as ever during the day, but they'd also clean up nicely and do daily transportation duty like no other truck ever could before. Studebaker wanted a Sunday-go-to-meetin' type of truck. Robert Bourke, Loewy's brilliant designer, did not disappoint.

"Studebaker sets a new truck style trend," bragged company ads announcing the arrival of Bourke's 2R pickup. "There is an unmistakable distinction about these new Studebaker '49ers,

which establishes new style standards for the entire truck industry. Look at them from any angle. Stand back for an all over view of their balanced proportions. Come close up and study the strong but graceful forms, the superior metal work. The unity of design in these new Studebaker trucks is as smart and as practical as that which distinguishes Studebaker passenger cars."

The 2R's alarmingly fresh face was enough to make it a true trend-setter. But what qualified the 1949 Studebaker pickup as a real milestone was the way in which Bourke tied it all together. This was indeed America's first fully styled modern truck. All that sumptuous sheet metal up front was complemented by rakish rear fenders that weren't just afterthoughts. Even though these fenders were still of the prewar pontoon fashion, overall impressions impressed like never before. The look was totally new: low and sleek and clean. This wasn't just a great-looking pickup, it was a great-looking vehicle. Period.

Too bad Studebaker was stuck with this timeless design until time ran out. Strapped for the cash to retool for another classic, South Bend execs were forced to build identical versions of the R-series pickup each year through 1953. And then all they could afford was a one-piece windshield and revised grille in 1954. The same beautiful body Bourke penned for 1949 was still around 10 years later. Studebaker pickups themselves became part of automotive history after 1964.

Had the 2R Studebaker been a Chevy or Ford, we'd still be talking about it today. Instead, whenever pickup milestones of the 1950s are mentioned, it is the two longtime leaders that get all the attention.

Studebaker's 1950 2R pickup was essentially identical to its all-new-for-1949 forerunner. But that wasn't all bad considering just how far ahead the company's styling was then. Studebaker was the first to both delete those old-fashioned running boards and integrate cargo box styling into a complete package.

Chapter 3

The Big Two's Big Two
Ford's F-100 and Chevrolet's Task Force

Simply describing Chevrolet and Ford as the two top-sellers in the 1950s truckmarket is like saying Marilyn Monroe was just a looker. Jayne Mansfield was a looker. Marilyn was... well, Marilyn was Marilyn. Until Dodge's recent rise in the 1990s, no pickup ever has enticed customers behind its wheel with anywhere near as much success as the Big Two have. Chevrolet has been America's best-selling truck maker every year since the late 1930s, and it continued to occupy the top slot with relative ease during the 1950s. Average yearly production from 1950 to 1959 was more than 313,000 units. The division's best effort came in 1950 when 414,496 new Chevy trucks were registered. Ford averaged 261,000 trucks a year, and its top number, 315,912, also came in 1950. Chevy's share of the market never fell below 32.5 percent; Ford's low was 22. More than 36 percent of the new trucks registered in 1950 were Chevrolets. Ford claimed its biggest slice of the annual pie in 1957 with 32.32 percent.

No other rival's annual production average even neared six digits. The closest any truckmaker came to the Big Two's brand of yearly sales success was International with 109,053 new registrations in the industry upswing year of 1959–and remember, International Harvester relied more on heavy haulers than its competitors. From a market-share perspective, Dodge cut out the decade's largest piece of third-place sales, 12.58 percent, in 1952. International's best, 12.35 percent came in 1958.

Domination is not a big enough word. Three out of every four new trucks registered in 1954, for example, were either a Ford, Chevy, or GMC. The Big Two blew the competition off the map. Nothing Dodge, Studebaker, International, or Willys could do would put a dent in that ironclad reality. Everything was in the Big Two's favor: history, brand recognition, numbers, you name it. Compared to their rivals, Ford Motor Company and General Motors had bottomless pockets. While Chrysler's wallet was by no means thin, it just never was able to make up the ground the Big Two had already covered thanks to their head start.

Of course cynics might point out that at least some of Chevrolet and Ford's rampant sales success during the 1950s could've been the result

While it was by no means faster than a speeding bullet, Ford's all-new 1953 F-100 pickup was indeed one super truck. It was even more comfortable and convenient to use than its Bonus Built predecessor.

Some historians consider the 1953 F-100 to be the first major turning point of the modern American pickup truck. It certainly represented the most extensive redesign effort of its day.

of a self-feeding phenomenon long common to the automaking industry. Who knows how many Chevy and Ford pickups were purchased simply because they were Chevys and Fords? Customer loyalty and trust (some of it blind) were also among the advantages held by the Big Two. Consider this: Chevrolet rolled out essentially the same Advance Design pickup for eight straight years and the model still sold extremely well; Studebaker tried selling its beautiful 2R truck for only five years and went down in flames for it. Of course it wasn't quite that simple, Chevy and Ford trucks sold so well primarily because they

were the two best trucks on the market, but you hopefully get the picture. In a perfect world perhaps the pickup market's pie could've been sliced more fairly, perhaps the Big Two wouldn't have been allowed to scarf up most of the pieces, perhaps the lesser makers wouldn't have been pushed away from the table. No one ever said, however, that life in Detroit was fair.

While South Bend execs struggled to stem the red-ink tide, their Chevrolet counterparts went to work each day with nary a care. They simply wound up their Advance Design pickup in 1947 and let it roll on into the record books.

The first F-100 cab represented state-of-the-art ergonomic design for its day. It was wide, roomy, and reasonably comfortable. Glass area was also enlarged to increase safety by enhancing visibility.

The first-generation F-100 was produced until 1956, when it was treated to a trendy, new wraparound windshield. This 1956 F-100 is also fitted with the optional Ford-O-Matic automatic transmission.

The 1950s were almost half over before Chevy designers finally freshened front end appearances in 1954. Their Ford counterparts, on the other hand, hurried to add a new grille to their F-1 pickup in 1951. Dearborn couldn't rest on its laurels if Ford was to ever catch Chevrolet again. Second was no place for the fallen leader.

Ford had risen to the top of the utility vehicle field not long after introducing its first truck,

the Model TT one-ton, in 1917. Chevrolet's legacy began the following year with its Model 490 half-ton. Ford then introduced the industry's first factory-built, steel-bodied half-ton pickup in 1925. A Chevrolet counterpart arrived in 1930. Chevrolet first wrestled the truck market crown from Ford in 1927. Ford then snatched it back in 1929. In 1930, Dearborn's market share reached a whopping 48 percent.

Ford finally replaced its venerable flathead V-8 with a modern overhead-valve V-8 in 1954. That "Y-block" engine in 1956 displaced 272 cubic inches and was rated at 167 horsepower.

Chevy hit 41 percent when it regained the lead in 1933. After dropping to second in 1935 and 1937, the Bow-Tie boys went back on top in 1938 and stayed there.

The race between the Big Two began looking like a runaway right after the war. While Ford's second-place market share came in like clockwork at about 21 percent each year from 1946 to 1949, Chevrolet's prime cut continually was on the rise: 26.8 percent in 1947, 29.2 in 1948, 35.9 in 1949. Ford's F-1 in 1948 couldn't erase the fact that Chevrolet was first with an all-new postwar pickup. That updated grille was no

help either. In 1950, the percentage-point gap between the top two spots in America's truck sales rankings was almost 9. The following year it hit 10. It was more than 11 by 1952.

Fortunately, Ford had more than a simple makeover in mind for 1953. This time copycatting Chevrolet wouldn't do.

While the F-1 was no slouch on its own, from the start it was destined to play second fiddle to Chevy's Advance Design. Chevrolet made the headlines in 1947; Ford only slightly rewrote the same story the following year. Dearborn officials not only needed to beat their rivals to the next

Chevrolet's popular Advance Design pickup finally retired early in 1955. In March of that year, the so-called first-series Chevy pickup was replaced by the all-new Task Force model. This 1955 first-series 3100 half-ton is fully loaded with optional exterior baubles, including full wheel covers, chrome grille with grille guard, and sun visor.

big punch. They also had to force Chevy's fiddlers into play. Simply catching the leader wasn't the goal; leaving the Bow-Tie behind was more like it.

Ford's attempt to do this resulted in the decade's first major milestone among pickups, the F-100. In many minds, the 1953 F-100 is the major milestone pickup of the entire 1950s, if not of all time. When *Automobile*

magazine named "The 24 Most Important Automobiles of the Century" in its September 1996 issue, included there along with the likes of Ford's 1908 Model T, the 1932 Duesenberg SJ, 1936 Cord 810, and 1945 Volkswagen was the first F-100.

"Every comfortable, driver-friendly pickup on the road today owes its existence to the original

Ford F-100," wrote *Automobile* founder David E. Davis, Jr., while explaining his somewhat surprising choice. "Until the appearance of the restyled Ford F-100 pickup in 1953, trucks were thought suitable only for commercial uses. But [the] F-100 was the first truck planned, styled, and engineered by a corporate management team, and suddenly pickup trucks became an alternative for personal transportation."

Ford's pickup revolution didn't come cheap. Dearborn accountants reportedly let loose their grip on $30 million for the F-100 development project, which involved one of Detroit's earliest ergonomic studies. If it wasn't in fact the earliest, it was certainly the most comprehensive to date. Designers were asked to take what had been learned earlier and create the safest, most comfortable, easiest-to-drive, hardest-working half-ton ever.

Chevrolet established all-new standards for style and flair with its Task Force trucks, introduced early in 1955. This 1955 3100 is dressed down with optional two-tone paint, full wheel covers and wide whitewalls. It's also powered by Chevy's milestone small-block V-8, which also debuted that year.

The 1955 Chevy pickup's newfound stylish flair was evident inside the cab. A nicely designed dash could have been complemented by an interesting array of optional upholstery treatments.

Stylists were put to the task with their goal being to incorporate all those functions within a form that would hopefully help change the way truck buyers looked at pickups. While the first F-100's body remained tied to traditional standards, it was certainly as easy on the eye as any light truck on the road. Most important, it was hands down more handsome, more refined, and more modern-looking than Chevrolet's aging half-ton shell.

The bulk of those 30 million bucks were spent on the F-100's "Driver Engineered" cab. New "driverized" features included improved instrument and control locations, sound deadener in the doors, an even wider seat than the F-1's with better shock-absorbing characteristics, and an enlarged, one-piece curved windshield. That latter trendy touch worked in concert with a new four-foot-wide rear window to produce a 55 percent increase in total glass area, all the better to help see and be seen. Extra glass meant added safety through better visibility. It also meant more style.

According to ads, the 1953 F-100 offered "more power, more comfort, more economy" as well. In the words of *Mechanix Illustrated's* Tom McCahill, the F-100's big new seat was "as comfortable as the average sedan's." This truck also drove more like an average sedan thanks to the steering wheel's relocation at a revised angle

Chevrolet's groundbreaking overhead valve V-8 was named the Trademaster 265 for truck use—and, yes, it was painted gray. Gross output was 145 horsepower.

A huge, new Panoramic windshield adorned the Task Force truck's cab. Further enhancing the view was the optional Panoramic rear glass shown on this 1955 Chevy.

to reduce driver fatigue. Additional steering improvement came from moving the front axle back (thus putting engine weight farther forward) to better balance the vehicle. This restructuring also reduced turning radius by about 19 percent.

More mechanicals included "The Greatest Transmission Choice in Truck History," as factory brochures put it. Along with a standard synchro-mesh three-speed, buyers picked from a three-speed with overdrive, a four-speed with grannie

low, and Ford's first truck-line automatic transmission, the Ford-O-Matic. Ford-O-Matic was only an option for half-ton pickups in 1953.

In 1954, the second-edition F-100 was treated to two new engines, the first being an enlarged, higher-compression overhead-valve six-cylinder. Displacement was 223 cubic inches, output was 110 horsepower. The really big news, however, involved the arrival of a modern overhead-valve (OHV) V-8, which finally superseded Henry's

Chevrolet's Task Force pickups rolled on in nearly identical fashion through 1957. Quad headlights were added the following year.

old, tired flathead. Horsepower for the new V-8 was 130, compared to 110 for the antiquated 1953 valve-in-block V-8.

The original F-100's career lasted four years, one less than the F-1's, an indication perhaps of the ever-growing momentum of the 1950s pickup market. Keeping up with the Joneses became more important as the decade rolled on. As far as catching up with Chevrolet was concerned, the F-100 didn't quite fill the bill. Chevy remained on top, with Ford on its heels, for another quarter-century. But the first F-100 did reverse a

downward slide. Ford truck sales in 1953 soundly shattered the company's previous record, set in 1929. Market penetration in 1953 jumped to 28.6 percent, fewer than 7 points behind Chevrolet. Chevy's lead fell to just 3 points the following year as Ford established another all-time sales standard on the way to reaching the 30-percent market-share plateau for the first time since World War II.

The 1953 F-100 not only helped Dearborn pick up the pace, it also inspired Chevrolet to do the same. By the time Ford added a modern

This 1957 Chevy half-ton is a 3200-series model or "long-box" truck. While the 3100 series rolled on a 114-inch wheelbase, the 3200 was based on a 123-inch stretch. Overall, the 3200 was 20 inches longer than the 3100. Also notice the optional "big window."

12-volt electrical system and an even more trendy wrap-around windshield to the first-generation F-100 in 1956, the company's groundbreaking pickup had been upstaged by Chevy's own historic half-ton. Ford in 1955 set its third straight sales record, again by a wide margin, yet still lost nearly two market-share percentage points to Chevrolet.

Chevrolet began the 1955 model year with its same old, same old Advance Design truck, which had been lightly updated in 1954 with a new grille and a one-piece, politely curved windshield. This was the division's so-called first-series model. On March 25, GM's price leader unveiled an all-new second-series pickup for 1955. Chevy's image-makers called it "Task Force." Critics considered it the decade's second great milestone truck.

1955 was, of course, a milestone year for Chevrolet all the way around. Its hot, new OHV small-block V-8 instantly ushered in a new age for the common car buyer. Chevy's stylish and graceful "Futuramic" car line offered a new standard of power and performance that had never before come this cheap. Much of what transformed Chevrolet's 1955 cars into the "Hot Ones" simply carried over into the truck ranks.

While a Task Force truck was nothing to sneeze at from an engineering perspective, its startlingly fresh face was what guaranteed its place in the half-ton hall of fame. Studebaker may have created a classic image in 1949, but it was Chevrolet that most emphatically announced the arrival of a new era in pickup design.

Chevy's second-series trucks for 1955 featured a newfound flair that reminded many truck buyers of a car-buying experience. Touches of car-like class were plentiful, especially in the headlights and grille, which were unabashedly copied from the 1955 Bel Air. Softened, sculpted lines flowed back from there with no interruptions as the previously used pontoon front fenders were traded for smooth walls of steel stretching from headlights to the back of the cab. Dodge in 1954 had first deleted pontoons up front, but its body still wore old-fashioned running boards below the doors. Like Studebaker pickups, Chevrolet's Task Force trucks no longer exposed their running boards.

Topping off the Task Force image was Chevy's "Panoramic" windshield, a decidedly car-like feature that "wrapped around" at the corners for maximum visibility and maximum style. Chevrolet in 1955 beat Dodge by less than a month with the pickup market's first wraparound front glass. And if that wasn't enough of a view for you, Chevy also offered an optional Panoramic rear window for the Task Force pickup.

A rainbow of exterior color choices were available as well. Thirteen solid shades were joined by 12 two-tone combinations. The latter signified yet another convergence of car and pickup styling trends. Just as it had demonstrated that low-priced automobiles no longer had to be dull, Chevrolet in 1955 showed us all that pickup practicality did not have to come in a plain wrapper, brown or otherwise. Dodge, International, and Studebaker also began leaving duller colors behind by avidly promoting two-tone pickup paint schemes.

Chevrolet dealers proudly played up their Task Force trucks through five model runs. Quad headlights were added in 1958, as was the Fleetside cargo box, a trendy slabsided copy of Ford's 1957 Styleside model, which in turn was a trendy slabsided copy of Chevy's 1955 Cameo Carrier. This country's top truckmaker was the leader of the pack in more ways than one during the 1950s. Ford may have been sittin' pretty at number two every year, but there was only one Marilyn, only one number one.

Chapter 4

The Best Of Both Worlds
Carlike Class Meets Truck Practicality

*H*ow soon we forget. In 1953, Ford's first F-100 was the greatest thing since sliced bread. It was the freshest, most modern pickup by far on the market—then. Time, however, waits for no one, especially in Detroit, where today's big news can become old news overnight. Pickup watchers only two years down the road were no longer looking the F-100's way. Chevrolet's Task Force trucks were now the main attraction, and rightly so.

Suddenly building the most comfortable and convenient, easiest-to-drive, toughest trucks out there was no longer enough. These same utility vehicles had to be really good looking too, almost as good looking as cars. In 1949, poor little Studebaker stepped out from the crowd with a truly stylish pickup and sent barely a ripple through the light-truck market waters. But when big bully General Motors tried the same trick in

1955, its dominating truck division was instantly declared the industry's styling leader. Might not only makes right, it also makes history.

Chevrolet's truck makers indeed made history in March 1955, first by raising the bar higher than ever for competing pickups to reach, then by pushing it out of sight. Dearborn officials' fading hope of holding onto any thunder was dashed when the Cameo Carrier was unveiled. This pickup wasn't merely a progression, it was an all-new approach that both left the past behind and redirected the future.

Just as the 1953 F-100 is recognized as a milestone for first helping transform the old workhorse half-ton into a daily driver, the 1955 Cameo deserves similar honors for demonstrating how well 100 percent car-like elegance could work in the pickup field. This high-class hauler was only around for four years, but its impact is

Rearward impressions of Chevrolet's Cameo Carrier were clearly carlike, which was primarily due to those attractive taillights and full wheel covers. Optional finishes were offered to Cameo buyers, but this 1956 model remains in the exclusive red-on-white paint found on 1955 Cameos. The non-stock dual exhausts were owner installed.

In 1955, all 5,220 Cameo pickups sold featured the same paint scheme: Bombay Ivory accented by Cardinal Red. Additional schemes were added each year during the Cameo's brief run.

still felt nearly a half-century later. Truck buyers at the turn of the millennium are spoiled; they automatically assume all pickups should turn heads like cars and play as hard as they work. Chevy's Cameo was the first to truly do so.

The genius behind the Cameo's creation was longtime General Motors design exec Charles M. Jordan. Jordan joined GM as a young apprentice in 1949 and worked briefly under Chevrolet truck studio chief Luther "Lu" Stier

before being called to Air Force reserve duty in 1952. While serving in a military art studio at Florida's Cape Canaveral, 2nd Lt. Jordan began dreaming of an entirely new light-truck breed. When not working on official assignments, he sketched various truly stylish pickups; sleek, sexy stunners that put most automobile designs of the day to shame.

Jordan the civilian returned to Detroit in 1953, and he brought his sketches along to show

Initial plans to form the Cameo's body out of steel in one piece (cab mated with cargo box) were shot down by budget constraints coupled with the plain fact that torsional stresses would wrench an integral cab/box body into a bent-up mess. Keeping the cab and box separate and molding the box walls out of fiberglass were the keys to making the Cameo dream a reality. This chrome strip then was used to distract eyes away from the typical gap then found behind a pickup's cab.

Another clever design trick involved the spare tire access in back. A center panel incorporated into the bumper hinged downward to allow the spare to slide out from beneath the bed.

Lu Stier. As luck had it, Stier's group at the time was busy sculpting the new Task Force image, so the door was wide open to fresh ideas. Stier loved Jordan's designs, as did Chevrolet chief engineer Ed Cole, the main man behind the new Corvette. Cole's support was also key to the Cameo's appearance, although that debut did not go as Jordan had planned.

Jordan's original concept incorporated two groundbreaking themes: flush, cabwide exterior bed walls devoid of the archaic pontoon fenders, and a one-piece cab/bed layout that allowed lines to flow smooth and uninterrupted from the grille to the tailgate. The scheme was certainly beautiful on paper. Real world possibilities, on the other hand, proved not so pretty. Jim Premo, Chevrolet's assistant chief engineer in charge of body production, immediately pointed out an obvious stumbling block. Torsional stress would surely warp all that super-clean sheet metal at the point where the

Although the same fiberglass-clad cargo box carried over each year for the Cameo, that box was treated to new two-tone paint in 1957. Wheel adornments also now featured center caps with bright trim rings.

cab and cargo box met, an inherent reality that explained why all pickups had separate cabs and beds to begin with. Game over, right? Wrong.

As Lu Stier later told *Special Interest Auto* editor Mike Lamm in 1978, "At that point, the division was practically ready to abandon the idea, but our studio insisted we could separate the cab and box without losing the desirable exterior appearance." Along with defeating a force of nature, Stier's crew was also able to beat GM's

bean counters, who had already determined that Chevrolet couldn't afford to fashion Jordan's stylish cargo box out of steel. "The cost of new tools and dies [would have been] too much for the projected low production volume," remembered Stier. His solution? "We were then able to convince the division that we could keep the existing stepside box and simply add fiberglass panels flush with the cab sides. We also added a fiberglass cover to the existing tailgate."

Quad headlights identify this Cameo as a 1958 model. Notice also the new "Apache" fender trim.

The idea was both simple and inexpensive. Using the existing cargo box and tailgate as a skeleton saved some serious cash. As for the fiberglass, molding was certainly cheaper than stamping steel, and Chevrolet already had a working relationship with the Moulded Fiberglass company in Ashtabula, Ohio. Moulded Fiberglass had been busy making Corvette bodies, but slow sales of Chevy's two-seat sports car left the Ohio firm with some extra time on its hands.

Those fiberglass cargo box walls were the stars of the Cameo show. A piece of chrome trim helped distract attentions away from the fact that there was still a gap between cab and bed. And graceful, car-like wheel openings complemented the crisp, clean lines. Additional "automobile-esque" touches included distinctive taillights and a unique rear bumper that incorporated access to the spare tire through a hinged center panel.

Once the Cameo's bed was made, completing the dream truck was no problem. Passenger-car full wheel covers were made standard equipment, as were Chevy's various Custom Cab baubles— chrome grille and front bumper, the full-width Panoramic rear window and extra bright trim inside and out. Although customers

From 1948 to 1953, Dodge tried luring customers back into dealerships after the snow melted each year with its high-profile Spring Special pickups. Stylish two-tone paint was the Spring Special's main claim to fame. This 1953 Spring Special, which also features Dodge's rare Truck-O-Matic option, was painted in non-stock shades of blue by its owner.

NEW *Golden Anniversary* INTERNATIONALS

International copied the smooth-sided cargo box idea for its all-new A-line pickups in 1957. New that year as well was a special Golden Jubilee model offered to mark the company's 50th birthday. Along with the cabwide Bonus Load box, the Golden Jubilee pickup also featured exclusive gold metallic paint.

could have picked either a six-cylinder or V-8, they had no choice as far as paint was concerned. An exclusive Bombay Ivory finish with Carnival Red accents was the only exterior treatment offered.

All this newfound prestige and pizzazz translated into an understandably high price for the high-profile Cameo. A car-like base sticker of about $2,000 was commonly quoted. This figure represented more than a 30 percent increase compared to a typical Chevy pickup's bottom line. It would have been enough to wilt the wallets of most truck buyers in 1955, but Cameos commonly were delivered to dealers loaded down with options with the intention of playing up the plaything ideal as high as it would go. Typical price tags reportedly surpassed $3,000 for Chevrolet's first pretty pickup.

Buyers apparently were not entirely intimidated by the Cameo's asking price. In 1955, production reached 5,220, a comparatively tidy total that qualified as reasonably large considering the vehicle's narrow-focused niche. Sales then predictably declined as the novelty wore off and rivals responded. Chevrolet discontinued the Cameo in 1958, but not before it inspired Ford to contribute additional momentum to the truck industry's slabside styling trend with its standard Styleside pickup in 1957.

International also got into the act with the smooth-sided "Bonus Load" cargo box for its new A-100 pickup, introduced in time to help celebrate the company's 50th anniversary. The Bonus Load box was showcased behind the cab of International's Golden Anniversary (or Golden Jubilee) Custom model, a Cameo knockoff of sorts. Along with its trendy box in back, this coveted A-100 half-ton also featured special trim and an exclusive gold and white metallic finish.

A much more famous Cameo copy came from Chrysler's truck division in 1957. By then, Dodge was in dire need of some serious sales promotion as the Big Two were quickly leaving it behind. And this was not for lack of trying. Dodge did many things right with its postwar pickups. In 1948, it was among the first to adjust chassis geometry to make its trucks handle better and drive easier. It jumped to the front of the pickup power pack in 1954 with its first V-8. That same year it also became the first to begin integrating front fenders into a cleaner, modernized cab construction.

Dodge was also experimenting with stylish two-tone exterior treatments before any other truckmaker dared to offer a pickup with a little flair. We're not referring to the standard Pilot House paint scheme, which included a black-only cargo box regardless of cab color—one solid shade from front to rear was a B-series option. From 1948 to 1953, Dodge offered a "Spring Special" package consisting of an eye-catching finish done up in contrasting tones for the pickup's upper and lower halves. The idea was to lure customers into dealerships with a splash of color each spring to help cure lethargic wintertime sales. Too bad Dodge officials gave up on such tactics when they did.

Dodge trucks made up a solid 15.43 percent of the market in 1946. It was still a healthy third-place player in 1952 with 12.58 percent. Then things began to slide. Dodge dropped below International into fourth in 1953 and slipped behind GMC in 1954. Market share dropped each year through 1958, when it bottomed out at 5.1 percent. Dodge remained in fifth for the duration of the decade.

Dodge designers didn't give up trying to keep up with the competition despite the downhill run, although diminishing cash flow after 1953 seemingly left them only able to address one area at a time. In 1954, a groundbreaking restyle added a trendy one-piece curved windshield. An updated cab featuring an even more modern wraparound windshield immediately followed in 1955. That cab then was adorned with a restyled nose in 1957. This same basic package remained on the scene up through 1960, a year in which Dodge's market share dropped even further, to a dismal 4.62 percent.

Efforts to stem this inevitable tide included a somewhat odd creation inspired by Chevrolet's successful combination of car-line class and pickup practicality. Dodge executives weren't blind; they could see how much the Cameo did to promote the new Chevy pickup line. But Chrysler's accountants obviously had far fewer beans to count than their counterparts at GM. The budgetary barriers Lu Stier's team had rolled the Cameo around in 1955 were peanuts compared to the sky-high hurdles Dodge designers needed to leap over in search of funding for a similar project in 1957.

Enter Joe Berr. Like Stier, Berr recognized that the best way to get where you wanted to go involved going around a road block, not over. He was a grade-A problem-solver—he had to be: he managed Dodge's Special Equipment Group (SEG). Custom modifications, primarily made for fleet sales, represented the SEG's reason for being. Driveline upgrades, reinforced frames, heavy-duty wheels and tires—whatever the special equipment, if it helped make a sale, Berr's group was ready to make it happen.

Joe Berr knew his way around custom orders. He also was well aware of his company's failing fortunes in the truck field. Dodge needed a shot in the arm, and it needed it fast if it was going to reverse its field. Simply freshening the front end would never do if the Dodge truck team truly expected to draw buyers' attentions away from all those attractive Fords and Chevys. Yet that was all the budget could stand in 1957.

Berr's contribution to his company's keep-up-with-the-Joneses campaign was both incredibly simple and conveniently inexpensive. First he pulled off those old-fashioned pontoon fenders from a new 1957 D100 half-ton. He then strolled over to Dodge's main assembly plant for a little sheet metal shopping. Berr returned with the bumper and a pair of rear quarter panels from a 1957 Suburban two-door station wagon. He gave these pieces to SEG man Burt Nagos, who welded the passenger-car quarters to the D100 truck bed in a flash. Presto, instant attention-getter.

Amazingly, the Suburban sheet metal, complete with its trademark fins and "traffic-light"

Dodge's response to the Cameo was its Sweptside model, which was introduced early in 1957. All Dodge pickups that year were treated to a restyled nose. This 1957 Sweptside is powered by the optional V-8.

Of course the stars of the Sweptside show were those unique tail fins, which were borrowed from a two-door Dodge station wagon.

taillights, fit like it belonged there, as did the station wagon's rear bumper. Once the car-line fuel filler was hidden and trim was added to the cab to match the Suburban's existing belt line brightwork, the only tough part of the operation involved cutting down the D100's tailgate to fit between those high-flying fins. Okay, those closing efforts appeared somewhat crude, but you couldn't blame Berr and his men considering what budget was allowed them. Sometimes nothing can go a long way.

"Straight out of tomorrow" was the description Dodge brochures used to announce the new Sweptside D100 pickup, which made its debut in May 1957. Adding to the standard attraction was two-tone paint, full wheel covers, wide whitewall tires and a chrome-plated front bumper. Early brochures listed deluxe cab treatments as optional, although it's highly doubtful that any of these high-profile pickups were put together in the SEG shop using a Spartan standard cab. Deluxe cab features included wraparound rear glass and full accouterments inside for both driver and passenger. Standard cabs were typically supplied with an armrest and sun visor only for the driver. Among additional options were power steering and brakes, the push-button-controlled Loadflite three-speed automatic transmission, and a 314-cid Power-Dome V-8. The yeoman 230-cid L-head six-cylinder power plant was standard.

Production figures for the Sweptside are not available, but its rarity is assured considering how low production numbers were for all Dodge utility vehicles in the late 1950s. New truck registrations reached only 49,431 in 1957, then slipped to 37,037 in 1958. Sweptsides were offered in both these years and were briefly built in early 1959 before being quietly canceled. Like Chevy in 1958, Dodge let its pricey, custom-built figurehead fall by the wayside in favor of a more conventional trend-setter better suited for mainstream sales. Dodge's 1959 smooth-sided response to Chevy's 1958 Fleetside was the Sweptline.

To market in style...

All-new '58 Dodge Power Giants are more

These four-way leaders of the low-priced three make your truck choice easier than ever in '58

Comparing before you buy a new truck is just sound business. This year especially—because there's a big difference between '58 models.

For one thing, only Dodge is really new. But more important is this fact: Dodge *Power Giants* now lead the low-priced three *all four ways*—

1. First in Styling. Striking new chrome grilles, smart dual headlights, and clean new lines mark these dependable, low-cost '58 *Power Giants* as the most modern trucks of all!

2. First in Power—in all popular farm models. New Super-Torque engines provide reserve power for more *pep* in traffic, more *pull* in mud and over rough ground. Also eliminates costly engine strain—cuts repair bills, lost work time.

Dodge offered the Sweptside pickup again in 1958 and briefly in 1959. New quad headlights were introduced that first year.

Dodge's intriguing Sweptside was quickly forgotten as the decade came to a close, a victim of the rapidly changing market that had ushered it in. But the idea that pickup buyers could have the best of the both worlds, that trucks could mix with cars, continued on to later become the rule, not the exception.

More Milestones

Truck Trends Pick Up the Pace

The American pickup truck certainly experienced its fair share of changes during the 1950s. Ford in 1953 made it more comfortable and more convenient. Dodge in 1954 made it more powerful. Chevrolet in 1955 made it more stylish. And all made it more competitive as the years rocked and rolled on.

Responding to rival advances became increasingly more important with the introduction of each all-new truck. For Chevy and Ford, this meant an ever-tightening struggle for the industry's brass ring. For Dodge, the game involved preserving what little was left of its Big Three ranking. For Studebaker, it was simply a matter of survival. For all, it was a matter of money. Those that had the cash to build a future had a future. Those that didn't, didn't. Of course Chevy, Ford, and even Dodge, with its sagging sales, had no worries. By the same token, International-Harvester wasn't concerned about its survival. Low sales in the pickup field were offset by the company's much more successful efforts with heavy trucks, construction machinery, and farm equipment.

Willys-Overland initially hung in there during the 1950s by doing one thing and doing it well. But the future of the world's leading 4x4 maker wasn't certain until it was bought up by industrialist Henry J. Kaiser in 1953, a transaction that guaranteed that at least the Willys name would carry on into the 1960s. Willys' postwar pride and joy, the Jeep, is of course still playing in the dirt today thanks to two additional purchases: American Motors bought out Kaiser in 1970, then Chrysler snatched up AMC in 1987.

Willys Motors, Inc. remained an individual subsidiary of Kaiser Industries until 1963 when it became the Kaiser-Jeep Corporation. But whether you called them Willys, Kaiser-Jeep, or just Jeep, the trucks that answered to these various names were unmistakable. The same basic durable, dependable pickup package rolled out almost unchanged from 1947 to 1963.

That's not to say that Willys wasn't a stranger to the 1950s truck market's cutting edge, however. Though few remember today, the 50-year-old firm from Toledo, Ohio, made a little history of its own in 1957. Willys' FC-150

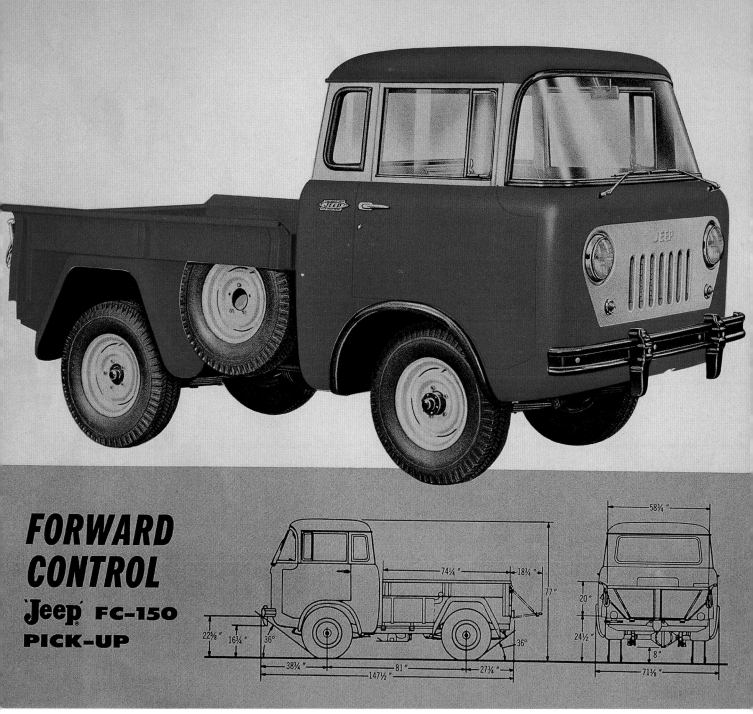

FORWARD CONTROL
`Jeep` FC-150
PICK-UP

Willys introduced a compact yet rugged pickup in 1957, the FC-150. The "FC" stood for "forward control," which meant the steering was located in front of the wheels. It was the forward control layout that allowed the use of a short, 81-inch wheelbase. A longer, heavier FC-170 was also introduced that year.

Dodge was caught in a "Catch 22" during the late 1950s. Fewer sales meant less money to invest in future development. When it came time to restyle the pickup line in 1957, only the very nose was made over. For off-road fans, the Power Wagon's scope was widened to include light-duty pickups. It wore standard sheet metal instead of the military-style body used by the traditional one-ton Power Wagons.

emerged that year as this country's first compact pickup. Although mini-pickups were then nothing new in America, the FC-150 best deserves this credit because it was a truck through and through, not a compact car with a minuscule cargo box tacked on in back like the tiny Bantams and Crosleys that came out before World War II. It was also a rugged, hard-working truck with a 5,000 pound gross vehicle weight, Willys' trademark 4x4 chassis, and a tidy 81-inch wheelbase.

The FC-150 idea involved combining the agility of the compact Jeep CJ with the cargo capacity of a full-sized pickup. Throwing in Willys' proven 4x4 hardware meant this little truck could

"go where others can't to meet your every need," as brochures claimed. Along with its off-road capabilities, the FC-150 also offered an incredibly short 18-foot turning radius, easily the tightest of any four-wheel-drive truck then on the market.

How did designers cut the wheelbase down to aid maneuverability while still keeping cargo capacity up near typical pickup levels? The "FC" in the name was short for "forward-control," which meant the steering wheel was mounted ahead of the wheels. Moving the driver farther forward allowed the use of a shorter cab, and a shorter cab translated into more room on the shortened frame for a reasonably lengthy cargo

New Styleside bodies—standard at no extra cost! Biggest in the half-ton field. New wider body makes side-loading far easier! Available in 6½- and 8-foot sizes.

FORD...America's lowest-priced pickup with cab-wide body*

Here's styling with a purpose! The sides of Ford's new Styleside bodies are built out even with the sides of the cab to give you up to 24% more load-space! Ford's Styleside is the biggest half-tonner built and it's standard at no extra cost!

But low first cost is only the beginning of the savings you get with '57 Ford Trucks. Modern Short Stroke engines, with new higher compression, are designed for low running costs. Rugged new durability features everywhere contribute to longer truck life. And the resale value of Ford Trucks is traditionally high.

For a truck that's modern through and through . . . for a truck that costs you less . . . see your Ford Dealer!

*Based on a comparison of factory-suggested list prices.

NEW **Cab**—new inboard cab-step, Hi-Dri ventilation! Roomier, stronger!

NEW **Ride**—all-new suspension with new rubber-cushioned springs!

NEW **Power Advances**—New higher compression! Only Ford offers modern Short Stroke V-8 *and* Six!

NEW **Super Filter Air Cleaner**—Stops 90% of dirt other cleaners miss!

NEW **Choice of** five half-ton pickups, including the new Ranchero!

NEW **Stronger Body**—welded, all-steel construction plus husky box-section corner reinforcements!

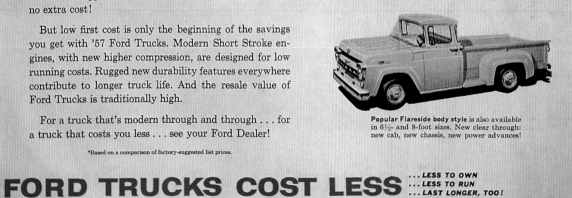

Popular Flareside body style is also available in 6½- and 8-foot sizes. New clear through: new cab, new chassis, new power advances!

FORD TRUCKS COST LESS
...LESS TO OWN
...LESS TO RUN
...LAST LONGER, TOO!

Ford in 1957 was the first to do away completely with the old-style pontoon fenders. Its new Styleside cargo box was also a no-cost standard feature. Customers stuck in their ways could still order the Flareside model with its rear pontoons.

INTERNATIONAL® A-LINE LIGHT-DUTY TRUCKS

International's move to modernize came early in 1957, just in time to help celebrate the company's 50th year building trucks. The "A" in the new A-100 pickup's name was short for anniversary.

International's new-for-1957 Bonus Load box was both functional and stylish. Its flush exterior walls fit in with the trend first popularized by Chevy's Cameo in 1955. And its cab-width construction allowed a few more cubic feet of cargo space to sneak in there.

box—the FC-150's box measured a shade more than six feet long.

While this "cab-over" type of design had been familiar to big rig drivers for years, Volkswagen was the first to offer Americans a forward-control pickup in the early 1950s. Willys translated this German ideal into its FC-150, which was also joined in 1957 by a longer, heavier FC-170 variant. Four years later, Ford's Econoline and

Chevrolet's Corvair 95 compact pickups copied the forward-control theme, although in lighter forms than their forerunner from Willys.

Willys Motors' FC-150 was just a single example, albeit one hidden by history, of how Americans were increasingly changing the way they looked at their trucks as the 1950s advanced. The trend-setting pace picked up in the decade's latter half. Progress early in the decade

Studebaker officials in 1955 were more than proud of their new V-8 option. Too bad the body it went into was the same one introduced in 1949. Both the one-piece windshield and grille insert shown here were new additions in 1954.

was comparatively sluggish because there was little need to race ahead to the 1960s, perhaps because market strategies even as late as 1950 were still very much akin to shooting fish in a barrel. Chevrolet's first postwar pickup stuck around almost unchanged for eight years after its 1947 debut and did so with little fear of ever falling from the industry's top spot. Ford's F-1 did a similar rollover run through five model years.

Studebaker never introduced a new truck during the 1950s, although the company wasn't resting on its laurels. Far from it: the veteran company's downward financial spiral left it with no cash flow to fund future development. Bob Bourke's beautiful body, unveiled in 1949, wasn't replaced until 1960. By then, it was too

little, too late. From 55,099 new truck registrations in 1949, Studebaker dropped to 10,192 in 1955, then bottomed out at 4,142 in 1958. An ever-so-slight resurgence, fueled only by a general upturn of the economy, followed in 1959, but later annual figures reached no higher than 5,900. A new grille and one-piece windshield in 1954 and two-tone paint in 1955 never had a chance of convincing pickup buyers that Studebaker wasn't stuck in the same old rut. The last Studebaker truck finally rolled off the tired, old South Bend line in December 1963.

Studebaker's fall from grace is not a story best detailed in 25 words or less. Rerunning the same pickup year in, year out alone was not to blame. But leaving buyers bored certainly didn't help. Such

8-foot pickup

½-ton 8-foot stake

new power . . .
new economy . . .
husky new truck styling too!

Count the superior features in these ½-tonners! Four engine choices: 170 or 178 h.p. Power Star 259 V8s; 92-h.p. Work Star 185 or 106-h.p. Work Star 245 Sixes Heavy duty 3-speed transmission standard with V8s; overdrive, 4-speed synchromesh, or automatic (V8 only) transmissions optional.* Exclusive Hill-Holder, power-brakes, Twin-Traction, and Deluxe Cab available as extra equipment.* Genuine hardwood floor with steel skid strips and channel rub rail in 8' stake body.

Model	Engine	Wheelbase	Pick-up	Stake	Platform
3E5 Chassis and Cab	92-h.p. Work Star 185 Six	112" / 122"	6½' box / 8' box	— / 8' body	— / 8' bed
3E6 Chassis and Cab	106-h.p. Work Star 245 Six	112" / 122"	6½' box / 8' box	— / 8' body	— / 8' bed
3E7 Chassis and Cab	170-h.p. Power Star 259 V8	112" / 122"	6½' box / 8' box	— / 8' body	— / 8' bed

Body Dimensions (Inside)—Pick-ups: 6½-foot, W-51½", L-78", H-17¼", 8-foot, 51½"x95¾" x 17¼". Stake: 8-foot, W-78", L-96¼", H-30¾".

Another revised grille in 1957 still couldn't mask the fact that Studebaker's Transtars were still Bob Bourke's babies behind the facade. The same could be said for the optional two-tone paint first offered in 1955, although this treatment did dress up what was already a classy-looking truck. Studebaker started labeling its light trucks Transtars in 1956.

CHEVROLET MODEL 3134—one of five dashing Fleetside pickup models! They come in a wide choice to suit many needs; maximum G.V.W.'s range from 5,000 lbs. to 7,300 lbs. . . . bodies in lengths of 78″ or 98″ (and a full 6′ in width) provide up to 75.6 cubic feet of load space. And you get 4-wheel drive with Fleetside models 3184 and 3684.

GOOD LOOKER, WILLING WORKER—that's the 1959 Chevrolet Fleetside pickup. That full-width tailgate is *graintight*, equipped with adjustable, rattle-free latches, and it's solidly constructed. Note the low loading height that makes your work easier. And the smooth-lined styling of those side panels will help build your business prestige.

In 1955, Chevrolet started the slabside trend with its Cameo Carrier, then translated what it began in fiberglass into steel in 1958. The sleek Fleetside model was also joined that year by the upscale Apache trim treatment. This is a 1959 Fleetside Apache.

repetition also distracted attention away from the valiant efforts South Bend planners made to try to keep pace in the 1950s pickup race. New mechanical modernizations included V-8 and automatic transmission options in 1955 and a four-wheel-drive model in 1958. Though these advancements also ranked as too little, too late, they did demonstrate that Studebaker wasn't going to simply dry up and blow away.

They were also indicative of the increasingly competitive nature of the light-truck market during the decade's latter half. Studebaker's engineering upgrades followed hot on the heels of similar motions kicked off by rivals intent on making their pickups more powerful, more convenient and overall more attractive to customers who seemingly each year were being treated to more and more new truck features. Ford's all-new F-100 in 1953 introduced optional automatic drive to pickup buyers. Chevy's and Dodge's first automatic transmission made their debuts in 1955. International's first automatic option appeared in 1957.

While Ford had been offering V-8-powered light trucks since 1932, the heart of these beasts was the valve-in-block "flathead," an engine that was obsolete by the late 1940s. Ford's first modern

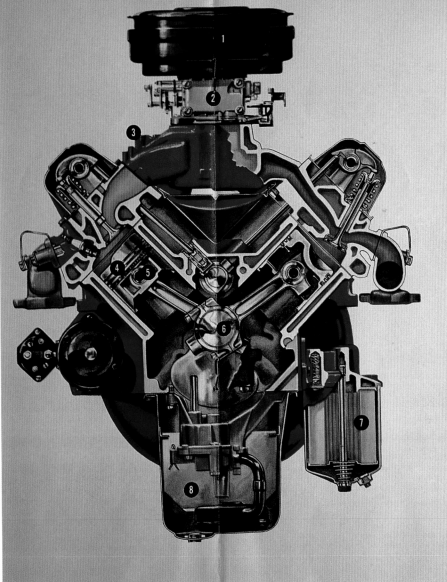

1. A large capacity, oil bath type air cleaner filters harmful dust and abrasives from the intake air.

2. The carburetor is a two-barrel, downdraft type of latest design.

3. The distributor is a combination vacuum and centrifugal advance type.

4. Pistons of thick dome type with upper rings set low, away from damaging heat, are reduced in weight and friction loss by elimination of excess metal from the side walls.

5. Piston pins, like other engine parts, are extra large . . . of true truck engine, not passenger car engine, design.

6. The crankshaft of forged alloy steel together with the flywheel and front pulley make a balanced unit assembly. This design makes possible a shorter, more rigid crankshaft and a shorter, smoother-running engine. Replacement of either crankshaft, flywheel or pulley does not alter the unit balance nor require special measures to restore it.

7. The oil filter is of familiar full flow type but larger in size and capacity than ordinary.

8. The deep sump oil pan prevents both under-lubrication and overlubrication of vital engine parts when the vehicle is greatly tilted from the horizontal.

• Timing gears are precision engineered with fine pitch gear teeth.

• A large-capacity, self-priming oil pump forces lubricant under full pressure from the floating, screened oil strainer to all main, connecting rod, and camshaft bearings.

• Dual large pulleys and dual belts are available for extra long life and economy.

International was the last to offer an optional V-8 for its light trucks, and it came in 1959. The lightly restyled B-series pickup that year could have been equipped with the V-266 engine, which displaced 266 cubic inches and produced 155 horsepower.

overhead-valve V-8 (for light trucks) was released in 1954, as was Dodge's leader of the horsepower pack. Chevrolet's first V-8 came out along with Studebaker's in 1955. International didn't begin offering an optional V-8 to half-ton truck customers until 1959.

By 1957, all truck makers were promoting driver-friendly power options. Chevrolet's first

power brakes and steering were introduced in 1955. That year Studebaker also began touting assisted brakes for its pickups. International's all-new A-series line for 1957 could have been fitted out with the works as well.

Options lists in general had begun to swell across the board after the F-100's debut in 1953, but Chevrolet's collection of extra-cost items for

its new Task Force truck line in 1955 was as extensive as pickup buyers had ever seen as many of the baubles car buyers took for granted began filtering across the fence in force. Deluxe doodads like full wheel covers, extra chrome trim, bright interior knobs, fancy-schmancy heater/defrosters, even fancier signal-seeking radios—you name it. All of this and more then started showing up in greater numbers at truck dealerships nearest you. The vast majority of pickups in the late 1950s remained trucks at heart—hardworking, no-nonsense machines. But the best of the breed got better each year as "fully loaded" took on an entirely new meaning for pickup owners.

Of course, added style wasn't overlooked either. Chevrolet garnered the most laurels in the 1950s for its up-to-date artistic touch. The sensational Task Force truck in 1955 had all its competitors—except Studebaker—rushing to their drawing boards to catch up. Such a challenge was imposing enough on its own, but Chevy's movers and shakers had to go and build their smooth, snazzy Cameo, and yet another trendy styling cue was soon sweeping truck country.

In 1957, Ford responded to Chevy's challenge with its startling Styleside. This new model not only deleted those archaic pontoon fenders in back in Cameo fashion, it also did the same in front, a look Dodge designers had been working on slowly since 1948. Conventional running boards disappeared as well, helping make the lower, wider 1957 Styleside the cleanest, most uncluttered pickup to date. Lines were concise and definitely uninterrupted. Styling elements were fully integrated from front to rear and top to bottom. Wags could make comparisons to refrigerators all they wanted, Ford's new-for-1957 truck body signaled the arrival of a new era for pickup design.

Ted Ornas and crew at International's design center in Fort Wayne, Indiana, also made moves toward that new era. In March 1957, they rolled out their A-series pickup to help mark International's 50th birthday. Along with a wraparound windshield, the A-100 truck featured a modern cab with overall cleaner lines. Fender tops were higher, the hood was wider and flatter, and running boards were gone. Pontoon fenders were still standard in back, but the optional Bonus Load smooth-sided box fit right in with the fenderless trend popularized by Chevy's Cameo.

Chevrolet even jumped back on its own bandwagon in 1958, introducing the steel-boxed Fleetside to pick up where the last Cameo that year left off. New quad headlights up front complemented the Fleetside's clean lines. And an equally new deluxe trim package called Apache further enhanced the appeal.

Chrysler's truck division was the last to join the thoroughly modern club, this after making various notable styling upgrades in 1954 and 1957. While that forward-looking front-end sheet metal continued essentially unchanged from 1957 to 1960, Dodge pickups were fitted with their own smooth-walled cargo box in 1959. Sweptline was the name Dodge label makers chose for their Cameo/Styleside/Bonus Load/Fleetside copy.

More rapid-fire styling changes lay ahead for the American pickup. Chevrolet and Studebaker were the first to help usher in a new decade with new trucks in 1960; Ford and Dodge followed suit in 1961. This time it was International that was stuck with the same body. Its next major restyle didn't arrive until 1969.

All that, however, is another story. For another time. About another decade.

After giving up on its slightly-off-the-wall Sweptside early in the year, Dodge in 1959 joined the rest of this country's trend-setting truck makers by rolling out its more conventional Sweptline pickup. *Courtesy Chrysler Historical Archives*

Chapter 6

Variations on the Theme
Cars That Worked Like Trucks

Chevrolet's Cameo Carrier in 1955 proved that Americans weren't opposed to mixing their trucks with their cars in the right degree. Two years later, Dodge demonstrated that perhaps blending in too much car with truck wasn't such a great idea. The intriguing, yet somewhat odd 1957 Sweptside appeared less like a forward look and more like one step beyond. While the Cameo is considered a milestone, a forerunner of today's warm-and-fuzzy workhorses, the Sweptside basically is not considered at all. It was an obvious knock-off, which didn't do this high-flying half-ton any favors from a historical perspective. Nor did the fact that the nameplate said "Dodge," which at the time meant that few pickup people were looking in the first place. The parent company's deflated popularity in the late 1950s virtually guaranteed a short run for the rarely seen, rarely requested Sweptside. It obligingly rolled into obscurity early in 1959.

Then again, Chevy's trend-setter was no iron horse either. Apparently having long legs is not always a prerequisite for forerunner status. As trend-setting as it was, the Cameo was history by 1958, after more than 10,000 elegant examples had hit the streets. Some might call that four-year total meager—for a mainstream machine certainly. But remember this truck was a window-dresser, a gate attraction intended to promote the Chevy's pickup image as a whole. Considering the Cameo's high price and limited nature, would you really want to get that pretty face dirty? Ten grand and out surely looked like winning numbers to GM's bean counters.

Dearborn's decision makers apparently didn't see things the same way. Unlike Dodge, Ford never concocted a direct response to the limited-production Cameo. Instead in 1957, the Blue Oval guys recreated some of the Cameo's appeal in the form of its mass-produced Styleside pickup. That

Instead of adding car features to a truck, Ford designers in 1957 opted to convert a car into a pickup. The Ranchero was created by basically stripping the roof off a station wagon.

Some critics in 1957 couldn't resist pointing out how the Ranchero's cab looked "sawed off" in back.

year Ford also created its own unique approach to the theme Chevrolet had originated in 1955. "Direct response" is the key term here. Ford's second new model for 1957 was a major variation on that theme. Chevy's Cameo was a truck that looked a little like a car. Why not, thought Dearborn designers, build a car that acts a little like a truck?

"For the person who has always wanted a pickup, but is balked by the looks or ride qualities inherent in normal trucks, Ford has come to the rescue," announced *Motor Life* while introducing the all-new Ranchero. This wasn't a promotional piece, or a mere novelty meant to lure bandwagon-jumping, fad-crazed 1950s

customers into buying "car-trucks." In the Cameo's case, the icing was the main attraction, not the cake. The Ranchero, on the other hand, represented a sincere attempt to offer customers the hardest-working car out there. According to *Motor Trend's* Walt Woron, it offered "the room and 'personal' feel of a Thunderbird, the comfort of a sedan, and the load-carrying capacity of a small pickup." Additionally Ford's promotional angle was purely self-serving—limited-production exclusivity wasn't the goal, relative sales success was.

Production of the first Ranchero hit 20,000, more than enough to convince Dearborn execs

All the comforts of a 1957 Ford passenger car were available inside the Ranchero's cab. Options included power seats and windows.

to keep it in the Ford lineup for a while. They wanted to see if a market did, in fact, exist for a car that worked like a truck. Longevity then proved that the half-car/half-truck combination was indeed a better idea from Ford. The Ranchero continued on uninterrupted until 1979. Early skeptics found faith in another form sooner than that. As Woron explained it in 1957, "I'll go on record with a proclamation that the Ranchero will be copied in principle by other manufacturers. It's too good to pass up."

Such validation came two years later from Chevrolet, which had the audacity to call its 1959 response "the brightest new idea of the year." Even its name, "El Camino," Spanish for "the road," was an obvious knock-off of Ford's south-of-the-border-sounding badge. But this time the copy overshadowed the original. El Caminos immediately outsold Rancheros, and Chevy's car-truck survived 27 model runs, although not consecutively. In 1961, the full-sized El Camino temporarily retired, then returned as an intermediate for 1964. Popularity quickly soared for the Chevelle-based El Camino, which was soon outselling its Ranchero rival, itself downsized in 1960, by at least a two-to-one margin almost every year. Chevrolet finally closed the tailgate early in 1988. By then, the

Except for its lower sidewalls, the Ranchero cargo box compared favorably with a typical half-ton truck as far as raw space was concerned. Hidden beneath that bed was the 1957 Ford station wagon's subfloor structure, complete with its unused spare tire location. Ranchero drivers had to keep their spares behind the seat inside the cab.

total tally (including GMC counterparts called Sprint and Caballero) read roughly 1 million. Ranchero's 23-year record added up to slightly more than 500,000.

Thirty years and 1.5 million vehicles—no one, not even Ford planners in 1957, could have predicted such a long and winding road for this unproven product. Initial hopes probably ran no higher than "let's go with this baby until it pans out." The first Ranchero, like its El Camino copycat, was approved because it was so easy and relatively inexpensive to build. Both multi-purpose machines were basically two-door station wagons with their rear roof areas peeled off to uncover the pickup-style cargo bays hidden below. Tailgates, of course, were also already there.

Because start-up costs were so minimal, it didn't matter if the first Ranchero found a market or not. Little would be lost, cash or face.

Fortunately, a market did exist, or perhaps it sprung up just in time to keep the Ranchero from falling flat. As *Pickups and Vans'* Spence Murray later wrote in 1972, "a need had been instantly created for a utilitarian, around-town light-duty truck with a sporty automotive flair.... Establishments that delighted in putting up a strong front grabbed Rancheros for one-upping their commercial rivals. Service stations wanted a fleet, handsome errand-runner, and repair shops and other trades felt a yen for a practical service vehicle that wouldn't be an eyesore among a background of high-priced passenger cars." Automotive

Chevrolet waited two years to follow Ford's "car-truck" idea with its El Camino. It immediately became the sales leader. It also survived nearly another 10 years after Ford retired the Ranchero.

press critics two decades before couldn't have agreed more, sort of. "Any company that needs a pickup could do much worse than advertise its name on the side of a Ranchero," concluded *Motor Life's* July 1957 report.

Chevrolet was a bit more specific when describing the new El Camino's target market in 1959. According to assistant general sales manager Albert Olson, Jr., Chevy's Ranchero response also responded to a newfound need on the West Coast for "a comfortable pickup." Among potential customers were wealthy, higher-brow buyers who were looking for a little

pickup practicality but still demanded certain levels of convenience, class, and style. Image-conscious businesses serving high-placed clientele were also targeted.

Whatever the real needs were, melding with the marketplace was a matter of time and testing for both Ranchero and El Camino. Ford officials had learned that bigger wasn't necessarily better because really big loads weren't what potential buyers wanted to carry. Spending big money apparently wasn't in the plans, either. The Ranchero survived into the 1960s only because it was repackaged in its more

Chevy designers also cut the roof off a station wagon to create the El Camino. But most critics felt their efforts to finish off the resulting cab were far superior to Ford's results.

affordable, much more compact Falcon form. Chevrolet gave its full-sized El Camino one more shot in 1960 before returning to the drawing board. Once established at the right size and price, both rivals then rolled on unquestioned through their long careers.

The Ranchero's roots date back to the early 1950s when a Ford designer drew up a new proposal as part of Ford's 1952 model-line restyle. These sketches mimicked Ford of Australia's popular "Ute," a half-breed utility vehicle that had been beating the bush "down under" since the

1930s. Around Dearborn, the name for this Ute spin-off became "Roo Chaser." Although it was first turned down, the Roo Chaser idea eventually resurfaced after Robert McNamara took over as Ford Division general manager early in 1955. It then became reality two years later.

True to its station wagon roots, the first Ranchero shared its tailgate, rear compartment subfloor, and wheelbase with Ford's 1957 two-door wagon. The Ranchero's 116-inch stretch between wheels was two inches less than the 1957 Fairlane's. Almost everything else carried over right down to those round taillights and polite fins in back. Obvious differences included the truncated roofline and pickup bed. Sheet metal stampings for the roof, upper cab panel, double-walled cargo box, bed floor, and tailgate inner panel were unique to the Ranchero.

Promotional literature called it "America's first work or play truck." Ford classed the Ranchero as a half-ton pickup and listed maximum vehicle weight at 4,600 pounds. The bed was eight feet long with the gate down, and storage volume was 32.4 cubic feet.

The base model went for $2,098, while the upscale Custom Ranchero, with its higher-grade interior and standard body-length trim borrowed from the Custom 300, was priced at $2,149. With that trim spear in place, Custom Ranchero buyers could order the optional Style Tone paint scheme. Eleven different shades were available for application below that spear, which complemented the Colonial White paint that went on top. Standard Rancheros only came in solid colors because they didn't wear any trim. That Custom Ranchero sales in 1957 nearly doubled those of its more mundane sibling perhaps demonstrated that the vehicle's appeal may well have involved more play than work.

Ford introduced the appealing new Ranchero to the public on November 12, 1956, in Quitman, Georgia, a rural community just west of Valdosta in the deep southern portion of the state. In a promotional ploy that day, a new

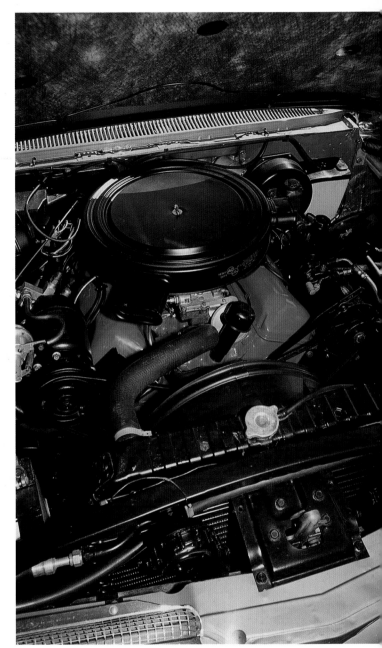

Like the Ranchero, the 1959 El Camino could be fitted with a wide array of power sources, beginning with an economical six-cylinder. The top of the line was this powerful 348-cid V-8. Beneath that big black dual-snorkel air cleaner are three two-barrel carburetors.

El Camino interiors could also be decked out with all the options available to 1959 Chevrolet passenger car customers. But in this case, the owner has added non-stock deluxe Impala upholstery.

1957 Ranchero was awarded to Wesley Patrick, who at the time was being honored by the Future Farmers of America as one of its "Star Farmers." While Dearborn officials saw Patrick as the perfect choice to first drive a Ranchero back to the farm, Wesley thought differently. He immediately traded his newly awarded pickup for a more conventional 1957 Ford passenger car. Luckily for Ford, 20,000 other Americans, country folk and city slickers alike, weren't so finicky.

Ranchero sales in 1958 fell by 50 percent, partially due to a national recession. Marketing strategies probably didn't help, either. Though it looked and drove like a car, the Ranchero was sold through Ford's truck division. Promotion also primarily came by way of truck brochures. Perhaps pickup buyers shouldn't have been the only focus, and Dearborn might have done better by also turning its attention to car buyers looking to have the best of both worlds.

Those who looked the Ranchero's way in 1958 found a fresh front end wearing Thunderbird-inspired styling. Rear treatments, however, looked quite familiar. The 1958 tail was a 1957 carryover. Incorporating the restyled 1958 taillights would have required splitting them in two astride the tailgate. That would have, in turn, meant running pesky weather-proof wiring into the gate to feed juice to the light's inner halves. Designers opted against this plan to save fuss, muss, and money.

Yet another restyle arrived for the last of the first-generation, full-sized Rancheros in 1959. A compound-curve (it wrapped around slightly at the top as well as the sides) windshield and a "floating star" grille were the most notable attractions. Wheel base was lengthened to 118 inches, and the bed was extended seven inches. Only one model, the Custom Ranchero, now priced at $2,312, was offered for 1959. Sales jumped up that year by 40 percent, but the decision had already been made to discontinue the

Ford's first Ranchero was known both for its economy, when equipped with the base 223-cid six-cylinder, and power, this thanks to two optional V-8s, one at 272 cubic inches, the other at 292.

full-sized model. The Falcon Ranchero was by then waiting in the wings.

Chevrolet thickened the plot with its first car-truck just as Ford was bidding farewell to its original. Introduced on October 16, 1958, the 1959 El Camino stacked up similarly with its three-year-old rival. Maximum payload was 1,150 pounds. The Ranchero's bed may have been longer, but the El Camino's was wider. Base price was about $2,350.

Critics gave Chevy the edge in the image department even though they weren't all that kind to the 1959 restyle in general. The running joke at Ford that year was that Chevrolet's new body resembled a "Martian ground chariot." Even styling chief Claire MacKichan later admitted that "we just went farther than we should have." MacKichan's team traveled the farthest with those horizontal tail fins, called "batwings."

Great new GET-UP . . . great new GO! New RANCHERO!

Ford's second-edition Ranchero was restyled up front but retained the 1957 tail. Designers apparently did not want to mess with splitting up Ford's new 1958 taillights across the tailgate seam.

Fortunately, many witnesses actually liked the way Chevrolet's out-of-this-world 1959 sheet metal fit the first El Camino. According to a May 1959 *Motor Life* review, those "gull wing fins blend in with the pickup bed better, perhaps, than they do with any other body style in the Chevy line." *Motor Life's* judge and jury also felt Chevrolet designers did a far better job of mating car with truck: "While the El Camino resembles a passenger car in every way, except for the short cab and stylish pickup bed, even the cab has rakish lines—more so than the Ranchero inasmuch as the rear window is not squared off but has a graceful forward slope."

Indeed, the first-generation Ranchero appeared like somewhat of a quick fix due to that flat-backed cab. The 1959 El Camino cab, in comparison, came off as an integral styling element. Its distinctive overhanging roof and sloping, wrap-around glass in back mimicked the "flyaway" roofline of Chevrolet's four-door Impala Sport Sedan. Minimal posts at the corners and a huge compound-curve windshield up front accentuated the airy "greenhouse" image. Remaining components were pure 1959 Chevy, save for the bed in back. A 1959 Brookwood station wagon donated the tailgate and rear quarter panels, and the long side spears came off a Bel Air.

Beneath the skin, the 1959 El Camino featured Chevy's rigid X-member chassis with coil springs front and rear. Station wagon rear springs and shocks were added to help haul the load. Even so, *Motor Life* reported considerable body roll in the turns and a noticeable squat with only 700 pounds planted in the bed. Optional heavy-duty springs were available to help prevent the rear suspension from bottoming out under load, but the trade-off was a considerable forward rake. While pickup owners were accustomed to this nose-down attitude, not all their counterparts on the car side of the fence would have been pleased.

Car owners, on the other hand, felt right at home with the wide array of optional equipment. Like its rival from Ford, the first El Camino could have been equipped with almost every passenger-car feature, including power brakes and steering, two-tone paint, deluxe interior appointments, and so on.

Power train choices for both Ranchero and El Camino were wide as well, from six-cylinder to V-8, from three-speed manual to automatic transmission. In 1957, Ford made it possible to install the Thunderbird's two top-performance 312-cid V-8s, one supercharged, the other fed by twin four-barrel carburetors. Chevrolet followed suit in 1959 with its 348-cid "W-head" V-8, the forerunner of the fabled 409. With three Rochester two-barrels, Chevy's hottest 348 big-block in 1959 put out 315 horsepower. Stuffed beneath an El Camino's hood, the 348 brought the bacon home in a hurry. Chevrolet even introduced a sport-minded four-speed with floor shifter in 1959, though very few were installed.

Performance, pizzazz, practicality—the El Camino offered it all, apparently more so than the Ranchero. About half as many customers chose the Chevy over the Ford in 1959—El Camino sales that first year were 22,246. The same wall that

DEMONSTRATOR SIGN on Ford Ranchero gets power from 1500-watt generator. '59 Ranchero (foreground) offers over 20 color choices. V-8 or Six. All power options, air conditioning

Big move forward in sign engineering, big move Ford-ward for eye appeal

"We make a new kind of eye-catching signs—and our eye-catching Ranchero helps sell 'em!"

"The Scintilite principle is something new in signs," says Rudolf Pabst, president of Prism Signs Inc., San Mateo, California. "These signs combine prismatic lenses with moving fluorescent lamps. Thousands of flashing lenses give new brilliance and animation to color patterns.

"We felt that a good-looking new product like ours deserved a good-looking 'showcase' Ford Ranchero. Like our signs, beauty to work for better business."

The new Ford Ranchero gives you the glamour and the go of the '59 Ford car, yet has full ton load capacity, is more spacious than ever. Says Rudolf Pabst: "When a salesman rolls to a prospect's place of business in a Ranchero and switches on the sign, the result is a double eye pleaser that captures attention every time."

Yet another Ranchero restyle appeared in 1959. The wheelbase was stretched and only the Custom model was offered that year, the last for the original full-sized Ranchero.

Dearborn planners had discovered loomed ahead for Chevrolet. Second-edition El Camino production for 1960 fell by 50 percent, convincing Chevy officials to also rethink their plans.

Both Ranchero and El Camino were reborn in the 1960s, reshaped to a point that caused many witnesses to quickly forget about these two unique utility vehicles' original forms. But they indeed were first a product of the 1950s, a time when Americans radically changed the way they looked at their cars. And their trucks.

Index